Paying for crime

Paying for crime

Edited by
PAT CARLEN and
DEE COOK

Open University Press
Milton Keynes • Philadelphia

Open University Press
12 Cofferidge Close
Stony Stratford
Milton Keynes MK11 1BY

and
1900 Frost Road, Suite 101
Bristol, PA 19007, USA

First Published 1989

British Library Cataloguing in Publication Data

Paying for crime.
  1. England. Criminal courts. Sentencing
  I. Carlen, Pat II. Cook, Dee
  344.205′ 772

  ISBN 0 335 09938 6
  ISBN 0 335 09937 8 (paper)

Library of Congress Cataloging-in-Publication Data

Paying for crime / edited by Pat Carlen and Dee Cook.
    p. cm.
  ISBN 0-335-09938-6   ISBN 0-335-09937-8 (pbk.)
    1. Sentences (Criminal procedure)—Great Britain. 2. Fines
(Penalties)—Great Britain. 3. Imprisonment—Great Britain.
I. Carlen, Pat. II. Cook, Dee.
KD8406.P39 1989
345.41′ 0772—dc20
[344.105772]   89-8763 CIP

Typeset by Burns & Smith, Derby
Printed in Great Britain by St Edmundsbury Press,
Bury St Edmunds, Suffolk

Contents

List of tables

Acknowledgements

We should like to thank Doreen Thompson, Secretary of the Keele University Centre for Criminology, for secretarial help with the editing of this collection, and John Skelton of the Open University Press for his usual support and encouragement.

Pat Carlen and Dee Cook

About the contributors

Hilary Allen, BSc, RMN, PhD, works as a psychiatric nurse and part-time lecturer at the Keele University Centre for Criminology and is currently engaged in research into elderly offenders. She has lectured and published on various aspects of law, psychiatry and gender, including 'Psychiatry and the construction of the feminine' (in P. Miller and N. Rose (eds) *The Power of Psychiatry*, Cambridge, Polity Press, 1986) and 'Rendering them harmless' (in P. Carlen and A. Worrall (eds) *Gender, Crime and Justice*, Milton Keynes, Open University Press, 1987). Author of *Justice Unbalanced: Gender, Psychiatry and Judicial Decisions* (Milton Keynes, Open University Press, 1987).

Pat Carlen, BA, PhD, is Professor of Criminology at Keele University and Director of the Keele Centre for Criminology. Publications include *Magistrates' Justice* (Oxford, Martin Robertson, 1976); *Women's Imprisonment* (London, Routledge & Kegan Paul, 1983); *Official Discourse* (co-authored with Frank Burton, London, Routledge & Kegan Paul, 1979); *The Sociology of Law* (ed., University of Keele, 1976); *Radical Issues in Criminology* (ed. with Mike Collison, Oxford, Martin Robertson, 1980); *Criminal Women* (ed. Cambridge, Polity Press, 1985); *Gender, Crime and Justice* (ed. with Anne Worrall, Milton Keynes, Open University Press) and *Women, Crime and Poverty* (Milton Keynes, Open University Press, 1988).

Dee Cook, BA, MA, PhD, is Lecturer in Criminology at Keele University Centre for Criminology and formerly worked for the Inland Revenue and DHSS. She has written various articles on the investigation and punishment of tax and social security fraud, and 'Women on welfare' (in P. Carlen and A. Worrall (eds) *Gender, Crime and Justice*, Milton Keynes, Open

University Press, 1987). Author of *Rich Law, Poor Law: Different Responses to Tax and Supplementary Benefit Fraud* (Milton Keynes, Open University Press, 1989).

Michael Levi, BA, MA, PhD, is Reader in Criminology at the School of Social and Administrative Studies, University College of Wales, Cardiff. He has published many articles on fraud and other aspects of policing and has written a Home Office guide to fraud prevention; he is author of *The Phantom Capitalists: The Organization and Control of Long-Firm Fraud* (Aldershot, Gower, 1981) and *Regulating Fraud; White-Collar Crime and the Criminal Process* (London, Tavistock, 1987). He has conducted research on police-public perceptions and on the costs of frauds for the Home Office.

Roger Matthews, BA, PhD, is Senior Lecturer in Sociology at the Centre for Criminology, Middlesex Polytechnic. Publications include *Confronting Crime* (ed. with Jock Young, London, Sage, 1986), *Informal Justice?* (ed. London, Sage, 1988) and *Privatising Criminal Justice* (ed., London, Sage, 1989). He has also written several articles on prostitution, alternatives to custody and decarceration.

Stephen Shaw, BA, MA, PhD, is Director of the Prison Reform Trust. He has written widely on both economic and criminal justice issues. Recent publications include *Conviction Politics: A Plan for Penal Policy* (London, Fabian Society, 1987); 'Prisoners' rights' (in P. Sieghart (ed) *Human Rights in the United Kingdom*, Human Rights Network, 1988); 'Law and order' (in *Public Domain*, CIPFA, 1989); 'A bull market for prisons' (in *Social Work and Welfare Yearbook*, Milton Keynes, Open University Press, 1989) and 'Privatising Prison Services' (in R. Parry (ed.) *Research Highlights*, Jessica Kingsley, 1989).

Peter Young, BSc (Soc), MA, PhD, is Senior Lecturer at the Centre for Criminology and the Philosophical Study of Law, University of Edinburgh and is Associate Dean (Postgraduate), Faculty of Law. He has written a number of articles on the sociology of punishment and the sociology of deviance. Author of *Punishment, Money and the Legal Order* (Edinburgh, Edinburgh University Press, 1989) and co-editor (with David Garland) of *The Power to Punish* (London, Heinemann, 1983).

Introduction

Pat Carlen

'The total amount of all those costs of crime which can readily be expressed in monetary terms is very large indeed, amounting to many billions of pounds a year' (Home Office, 1988c: 2). Additionally there are the costs which cannot be expressed in monetary terms: loss of life, limb and property; the psychological damage resulting from domestic violence, rape and sexual assault in particular and other crimes in general; and multiple fears of crime which increasingly inhibit and atrophy the enjoyment of public space and transport in many urban areas (see Jones *et al.*, 1986). Nor are these fears of crime without foundation. In 1987 the total number of crimes recorded by the police in England and Wales was 3,892,200 (Home Office, 1988c: 8) with ' "crimes of violence against the person" and "sexual offences" amounting to about 5% of the total and criminal damage to property about 15%' (Home Office, 1988c: 8). The other 80 per cent consisted largely of thefts, burglaries and frauds. However, and as is pointed out in the 1987 *Criminal Statistics: England and Wales*,

> *The British Crime Survey* (Hough and Mayhew, 1983) shows that, for the sum of offences in categories which can be compared to those recorded by the police, the amount of actual crime committed is perhaps four times the number of crimes recorded by the police.
> (Home Office, 1988b: 19)

Over the ten years since 1977 the increase in recorded violence against the person has averaged 7 per cent per year (ibid: 21) and in recorded burglaries 4 per cent per year (ibid: 22). In offences of fraud and forgery since 1980 'the recorded total has [also] increased by an average of 4 per cent per year' (ibid: 24) . . . and so on. As crime increases so do its costs. Who, then, foots the bill? Ultimately, of course, we all do, though the most immediate costs are borne by crime victims, by the state and (both metaphorically and materially) by offenders themselves.

According to *Criminal Statistics: England and Wales* (Home Office, 1988b) the values of recorded stolen property in 1987 were: burglary in a dwelling – £272 million; burglary other than dwelling – £187 million; robbery – £37 million; theft from vehicle – £120 million; theft of motor vehicle – £662 million; and other theft – £191 million (quoted in Home Office 1988c: 13). Though it should be noted that

> in practice, measurement is complicated (a) by the question of whether the property stolen was insured and whether a claim was made; and (b) whether it was recovered and returned to the owner, and if so, when and in what state?
>
> (Home Office, 1988c: 13)

The costs of violent crimes – though a monetary value *is* put on injuries by the Criminal Injuries Compensation Board (CICB): see below – are even more complex. Emotional and mental scars may affect the victims' work and social performance long after the physical wounds have healed. Fear of crime in the streets or in the home reduces the quality of life for many poorer people and increases the cost of living for richer citizens as they invest in expensive security devices to protect their lives and property. Yet though all victims of violent and property crime suffer some loss it is important to note that

> the less well off the victim, the greater the proportionate financial effect of a loss of any given amount, the less likelihood that the loss will be covered by insurance, the less the ability to cope with any consequential loss and inconvenience – and the greater likelihood that the victim cannot afford the kind of physical protection which might have prevented the crime in the first place.
>
> (Home Office, 1988c: 14)

Once the costs of crime to commercial and governmental department victims (e.g. Inland Revenue) are added to those accruing to individual victims, the price we pay for crime can be seen to approach phenomenal levels. 'For example, the largest fraud victim in the U.K., which is the Treasury, is cheated out of what is "guesstimated" to be some £5,000 million annually' (Home Office, 1988c: 18). Yet the costs of crime are not only borne by the state when its administrative bureaucracies fall victim to crime. Further costs are incurred in the compensation of victims and the prevention, policing and punishment of criminal offences.

In 1987/8 the Criminal Injuries Compensation Board paid a total of £52,042,581 in compensation to victims in England, Wales and Scotland, while the scheme's actual administrative costs came to £6,759,855 (Criminal

Injuries Compensation Board, 1988: 7). Other costs of crime paid for by the state include

1 *The police*: the overall cost of the police in England and Wales in 1987 was £3,500 million (Home Office, 1988a).
2 *The Crown Prosecution Service*: its expenditure in England and Wales in 1988/9 was estimated to be £170 million (ibid.)
3 *Legal aid in criminal cases*: in England and Wales in 1986/7 it cost about £200 million (ibid.)
4 *Criminal courts*: 'Expenditure on the Crown Court (excluding legal aid and on the magistrates' courts) in 1986/7 was £144 million and £179 million, respectively' (ibid.). (Figures for England and Wales only.)
5 *Probation service*: 'the total cost of the service in the financial year 1986/7 was approximately £215 million' (ibid.). (Figures for England and Wales only.)
6 *Prison service*: 'in 1986/7 £698 million was spent on the prison service in England and Wales' (ibid.).

The Home Office, the Department of the Environment, local authority social service departments, crime prevention schemes, Port, Harbour, Dock, Railway and Airport Police Forces, as well as voluntary bodies (and criminologists), also incur substantial costs in the prevention of crime and the management, policing (and researching) of offenders. In fact, as the institutions involved in crime control are totted up, a cynic might begin to suspect that crime is keeping a great many law-abiding people in business, and that it's not only corporate and professional criminals who make a good living from villainy. Cynicism aside, though, to individual victims, offenders and sentencers crime is certainly no laughing matter. Victims pay the price of crime with loss of their health, property and, very occasionally, physical or mental capacity or lives. Offenders pay by suffering punishments designed (variously) to be denunciatory, retributivist or restitutive and (ideally) weighted according to the seriousness of the offence. Sentencers try to juggle with the contradictory demands of complex and penal philosophies to achieve – what? Real or symbolic recompense for victims of crime? 'Just deserts' for criminals? Protection of society? Or a reduction in crime in the future?

In this book we will examine the jurisprudential and practical sentencing problems currently confronting magistrates and judges. Our starting-point is an assumption that in a society where income differentials are widening and monetary penalties the most usual punishments favoured by the criminal courts, it is not surprising that sentencing dilemmas have been exacerbated in the 1980s by the increased levels of poverty and unemployment. The major arguments will be that although of course 'something must be done' about crime we should also re-examine contemporary sentencing myths that assume it is only in relation to the poor that sentencing paradoxes arise, see custody as the necessary and inevitable back-up to the non-custodial penalties, and assume that the only viable alternatives to imprisonment are those transcarceral ones that bring the pains of imprisonment into the already straitened circumstances of the poor outside prison. The book's overall practical aim is identical to that described by Hilary Allen as being the specific objective of Chapter 4: 'to demonstrate . . . that there are intelligible alternatives to some of the more unthinkingly punitive practices of current sentencing' (p. 66). It is essential that these alternatives are taken seriously for three important reasons, all of which were concisely stated in the 1988 Green Paper *Punishment, Custody and the Community*. First, because

> if they [offenders] are removed in prison from the responsibilities, problems and temptations of everyday life, they are less likely to acquire the self-discipline and self-reliance which will prevent re-offending in the future. . . . Imprisonment is likely to add to the difficulty which offenders find in living a normal and law abiding life. Overcrowded local prisons are emphaticially not schools of citizenship.
>
> (Home Office, 1988a: 1–2)

Second, 'if offenders remain in the community, . . . they should be able to make some reparation for the harm they have done' (ibid.). Third, 'punishment in the community should be more economical on public resources. On average, holding someone in prison for a month costs twice as much as the average community service order' (ibid.). In fact 'in the financial year 1986/7, the average cost of keeping a person in prison was £252 per week' (NACRO, 1988a) whereas by comparison the costs of other penal measures were as follows:

> *Probation orders*: in 1985/6 the estimated annual cost of supervising an offender on probation was £780 [Home Office, 1987a].
> *Community service orders*: in 1985/6 the average annual cost of supervising an offender on a community service order was some £690. The cost of each order averaged some £450 [Home Office, 1987b].
> *Attendance centres*: the average cost of an attendance centre order in 1986/7 is estimated to have been about £108 [parliamentary answer from Earl Ferrers to Lord Donaldson, *Hansard*, 14 March 1988, col. 1022 . . .].
> *Probation hostels*: in 1986/7 the estimated average annual cost of a place in an approved probation hostel was £8,095 [parliamentary answer from Earl Ferrers to Lord Donaldson, *Hansard*, 14 March 1988, col. 1022].
> *After-care hostels*: the average Home Office grant towards the cost of a voluntary after-care hostel for offenders is about £1,000 per year per place [parliamentary answer from John Patten MP to Charles Irving

MP, *Hansard*, 14 July 1987, col. 412].
(All figures and sources referred to are from NACRO, 1988a)

Chapter 1 of this book is primarily concerned with presenting an overview of the main jurisprudential and practical difficulties confronting courts when they try to impose just sentences on offenders of widely differing means. After presenting three dominant models of sentencing logic, the author argues that the government's recent proposals for punishment in the community will only work if based on a fourth model – State-obligated Rehabilitation – and that a central assumption of this model would be that the main objective of all sentencing should be the reduction of crime without an increase of inequality, i.e. that generally there should be no imposition of any sentence which, given the offender's income or social circumstances, would certainly increase social inequalities still further. It is also suggested in Chapter 1 that 'sentence feasibility' should be promoted as a major sentencing principle.

Although *Paying for Crime* is concerned with both custodial and non-custodial sentences, a great deal of it is devoted to filling a gap in the existing literature by examining that most common of all penalties – the fine. For as Stephen Shaw points out in Chapter 2 (where he gives an authoritative overview of the research on fines, fine default, and alternatives to sending fine-defaulters to gaol),

> despite the fact that the fine is overwhelmingly the most common penalty employed by the English courts, the literature on fines and fine default is not extensive. . . . Given that in the region of 1.5 million fines are passed by the courts each year, one wonders if there can be any other such common-place experience which has so escaped the attentions of research.

Moreover, just as little attempt has been made to solicit the views of offenders who have been fined, so have there been few attempts to seek out the views of the sentencers with whom the fine has traditionally found such favour.

The models of sentencing logic discussed in Chapter 1 are ideal-types, constructed from government exhortations to sentencers as to how they should assess cases; they are not rooted in sentencers' own descriptions of the logic they actually employ in court. Indeed, very little is known about judicial and magisterial ruminations at this point of sentence. That is why Peter Young's recent work on the history and use of the fine in Scotland is so important (P. Young, 1988). Some of that research is now reproduced in Chapter 3, where Young draws on material from interviews with sheriffs in three cities in central Scotland to present a fascinating account of how they rank competing objectives such as punishment, treatment and expediency and then attempt to balance them against each other when determining the actual level of fine appropriate in specific cases. Yet, despite elements of individualization in their reasoning, the Scots sheriffs interviewed held a predominantly classical view of criminal justice. That is, their main concern was that the sentence should be proportionate to the offence. Information about the offender was assigned a subordinate status and was considered to be relevant mainly in relation to the offender's record. In other words, sheriffs saw themselves as using the justice model of sentencing (see p. 47) in conjunction with the 'tariff' – the sentencing system based on the notion that there is a hierarchy of punishments (ultimately leading to, and all backed-up by, imprisonment) and that each time offenders are convicted they should receive that sentence which is one higher on the 'tariff' than the last sentence served.

The explicit emphasis on 'just deserts' and the desirability of 'tariff' sentencing is a rhetoric embraced by many British sentencers and its implementation has undoubtedly contributed to the push-pull flow of increasing numbers of offenders into the prison. Yet, in the cases of certain groups of offenders, sentencers systematically employ a logic which subverts the 'tariff'. Nowhere can this be seen more clearly than in the cases of black offenders (see Chapter 1), some female offenders (see Allen, Chapter 4) and some categories of fraudsters (see Levi, Chapter 5). In the case of black offenders subversion of the 'tariff' appears to work entirely to their disadvantage and they seem likely to receive harsher sentences than whites convicted of the same offence and with similar records (see NACRO, 1986a). For women the sentencing logic is more complex – with some types of 'respectable' or 'mentally ill' offenders receiving very lenient sentences for quite serious crimes (see Allen, 1987; Chapter 4 in this volume) and other, less 'respectable' women receiving prison sentences for very minor crimes indeed (see Carlen, 1983b; 1988; Allen, 1987). Finally, and as Mike Levi demonstrates in his careful analysis of the sentencing of business criminals, 'there is a common mode of rationality from which white-collar defendants benefit, and benefit considerably, compared with those few offenders who steal sums as substantial as do fraudsters' (Levi, Chapter 5: 105). Yet as Dee Cook argues in Chapter 6, where she describes and explains the differential treatment of tax and welfare fraud, these common modes of rationality, which systematically subvert the logic of 'just deserts' and 'tariff' sentencing in the case of certain categories of offender, are not peculiar to magistrates and judges. Rather they are constituted within dominant political, economic and ideological discourses that make it possible to attribute entirely different motives and meanings to the crimes of people already differentiated from each other by the structural effects of class, gender and racism.

Now, one conclusion which might be drawn from the detailed work on sentencing by Allen and Levi is that if we can already deal with certain groups of serious offenders by non-custodial means, then surely we should examine the logic in use in such cases with a view to extending it to other groups of offenders (see Carlen, 1989). For instance, *the whole distribution of female disposals should be taken into account in every review of sentencing policy.* This distribution should lend weight to existing arguments which suggest that in many cases imprisonment could be safely avoided altogether, and punitive sentences replaced by more lenient and rehabilitative ones.

(Allen, Chapter 4: 84)

In order for such comprehensive review to occur it would be necessary to have some kind of central review body like the Sentencing Council proposed by Andrew Ashworth in 1984 (Ashworth *et al.*, 1984), as well as a ministry of justice concerned with developing coherent sentencing and penal policies.

But sentencing reforms are not enough, and in Chapter 7 Roger Matthews concludes this volume of essays by arguing that if we are to control crime we also need to take prison reform seriously. It is difficult to foresee a time when it will not be necessary to contain in custody those individuals whose behaviour makes them too dangerous to be left at large. None the less, the contemporary conditions in our prisons are not conducive to changing offenders' behaviour for the better. Just the reverse. In Chapter 7, therefore, Matthews draws upon a range of research studies from abroad to support his conclusion that, given the political will, we could still turn the rehabilitative 'ideal into a reality'. It would certainly be the most cost-effective way of paying for crime.

1
Crime, inequality and sentencing

Pat Carlen

Mass unemployment, together with the increased inequality produced by the interaction of government policy on wages, taxes, benefit and wealth has meant that:

the proportion of original income received by the poorest fifth of households in 1985 had fallen to little more than a third of its 1979 level – the result largely of unemployment;

the original income share of the poorest 40 per cent had fallen by more than a third: reflecting the combined effect of unemployment and low pay;

in contrast the top fifth of households had seen their income share rise by an average 10 per cent.

(Byrne 1987)

Introduction

The striking increase in inequality of income and wealth which has been a major feature of the last decade (Walker and Walker, 1987) has been accompanied by a steady increase in the prison population from 41,800 in 1978 to over 50,000 in 1988 (Home Office, 1988a). This is not surprising. Whatever else prisons may be for, they have always housed large numbers of the poor, the unemployed, the unemployable, the homeless, the physically ill and the mentally disturbed. From time to time, also, these staples of the prison population have been augmented by large contingents of other 'problem' populations such as ethnic minority groups, political protesters and, most noticeably in recent years, unemployed *youth*. And, as commentary on the blatant inequities of the criminal justice system, one constant jurisprudential theme has persistently centred upon the impossibility of imposing a system of formal justice (predicated upon an assumption of equality before the law) upon a system of substantive inequality. Nor has this concern about the relationship between criminal justice and social justice been merely academic. In the courts sentencers have daily wrestled with the problems of sentence feasibility (how to punish someone who has not the wherewithal to pay a financial penalty, or who is already living in excessively punishing social conditions); and equality of sentence impact (how to impose similar degrees of penal pain or deprivation upon offenders of differing sensibilities or material means). Recently these sentencing dilemmas have become even more acute as magistrates and judges have been exhorted by government – variously – to get tough with offenders; to send fewer people to prison; to be realistic in their choice of penalties. In order therefore to elucidate some of the sentencing dilemmas and paradoxes that arise in a society where inequality is increasing, this opening chapter will

1 discuss the relationships between inequality, crime and punishment
2 outline four different models of sentencing
3 assess those models according to their capacity to develop effective measures of penal intervention without increasing inequality and its effects still further.

The fundamental implication will be that, until there is a greater recognition of the relationships between crime, criminal justice and social justice, it is unlikely that sentences will be fashioned which will bring about reductions in lawbreaking. At the most general level the argument will be that the state's right to punish is based on a contractual obligation to attempt to rectify the particular 'social problems which both occasion, and are occasioned by, lawbreaking' (Carlen, 1983a: 213) and that forms of punishment which ignore that obligation, while they might fulfil other functions, will *not* reduce crime. More specifically it will be argued that there is an urgent need to re-examine the contemporary penality that

1 continues to insist that responsibility for lawbreaking lies totally with individuals who have an unfettered choice as to whether or not they break the law
2 assumes that it is only in relation to the young and the poor that sentencing dilemmas arise
3 privileges the 'tariff' as a major guide to sentencing
4 sees prison as the necessary and inevitable back-up to non-custodial penalties

5 assumes that the only viable alternatives to imprisonment are those
   transcarceral ones that bring the pains of imprisonment into the already-
   straitened circumstances of the poor outside prison
6 allows sentencers greater independence than their collective wisdom most
   probably warrants.

Inequality and crime

Having reviewed sixteen major studies of the relationships between income
inequality and crime, Steven Box concluded in 1987 that 'income inequality
(rather than poverty alone) is strongly related to criminal activity' (Box,
1987: 96) and that during the recent recession there was an increase both in
conventional and white-collar crime (Box, 1987: 98–102). What's more, an
earlier analysis of unemployment and *imprisonment* conducted with Hale
had already shown a virtual consensus that 'unemployment is related to
imprisonment independently of the crime rate' (Box and Hale, 1985). In
Box's and Hale's own study, *even after they had excluded fine defaulters*, a
significant relationship between unemployment and imprisonment was still
apparent, a relationship, moreover, that could not be totally explained by
changes in crime rates. But why has the recession of the 1970s and 1980s
been accompanied by an increase in crime rates and a quite disproportionate
increase in imprisonment?

   It is often argued that if unemployment causes crime we could have
expected the crime rate of the 1930s to have been similar to that of the 1980s.
Instead, and as Lea and Young (1984: 90) point out, although 'the amount
of unemployment in 1933 and 1981 was roughly equal (around 11.5 per
cent), the amount of serious crime per 100,000 population in 1981 was over
fifteen times as great as that of 1933.'

   The ideological and political conditions of the 1980s are very different to
those of the 1930s. Whereas the majority of unemployed in the 1930s were
people who *had* experienced work and hoped to be employed again,
unemployment today is concentrated amongst the young who have never
known the rewards of work and who have little reason to believe that those
rewards will be forthcoming in the future. Furthermore, today's unemployed
have had their expectations of what they *should* receive by way of material
rewards raised way beyond those of their grandparents. These higher
expectations were initially raised by the short-lived 1960s economic boom
and universal education, and have most recently been fuelled by daily mass
media references to a world of plastic money and city financiers' six-figure
salaries. Yet between 1976 and 1985 when the share of original household income of the top 20 per cent was rising from 44.4 to 49.2 per cent,
the share of the bottom 40 per cent fell from 10.2 to 6.3 per cent (National
Children's Home, 1988: 8). During that same period unemployment
trebled (ibid: 9). and by 1986 120,000 households were homeless, with

72,000 of the latter having one or more dependent children (ibid: 10).

At the same time as the poor were getting poorer (and prison), and more marginalized people who in any case were not getting their 'just deserts' were choosing to break the law, more and more of the business community, spurred on by the competitive individualism (greed) of a free market economy, also came to believe that the 'market' was somehow letting them down, and that they were therefore entitled to engage in financial crimes. (See Levi, 1987: 5 on the 5 per cent annual increase in recorded fraud since 1980.) In many ways theirs was a rational choice. For though it might seem that the wealthy have much to lose by lawbreaking, the slim chances of their being caught, prosecuted and convicted, combined with the often dispersed sources of their income and wealth, means that they can usually make the accurate calculation that in their own cases, at least, crime *does* pay. A similar calculation cannot so rationally be made by the majority of wage-earners and unemployed. However, under certain circumstances – for instance, rising unemployment and government policies that far from bolstering the 'family' and other types of households, actually attack and weaken them to such an extent that they become the sites of increased violence – under those circumstances, increasing numbers of politically and economically marginalized people feel they have less to lose and more to gain by committing crime (cf. Kornhauser, 1978). Once they do commit offences, the effects of certain sentences – especially imprisonment – result in their options being narrowed still further. Thereafter, whichever way they turn, they seem to come up against an official blockade of all legal routes out of poverty.

Examples of this narrowing options syndrome (Rosenbaum, 1983) were apparent in a recent small study of thirty-nine recidivist women criminals (Carlen, 1988). Several had enjoyed and successfully completed Youth Training Schemes – before being slung back into unemployment at the end of the year. No fewer than six had been involved with volunteer organizations engaged in various community projects – until cuts in local authority funding had closed them down. Many had gained some educational qualifications while in prison – and had found upon release that these were absolutely useless to them as far as employment prospects were concerned. And so on – until the combination of poverty and a narrowing of *options* for escape from it had made them believe that the only way in which they *could* take control of their lives was to commit crime. Conversely, those who had given up crime had done so not primarily through fear of another custodial sentence, but because of a change for the better in their circumstances. Their own resolve to turn their backs on crime had been a necessary but insufficient condition for their changed life-styles. It had been the 'good' probation hostel, the flat, the job, the good friend or a newly found financial security that had enabled them to turn resolution into reality. This is neither new nor surprising. As Barbara Hudson has said:

Although there is rarely consensus in the criminological field it is more or less accepted as 'folk wisdom' that rather than being deterred from recidivism by anything that might be visited upon them by the agents of social control, people give up crime when they acquire bonds to the social order. . . . It could well be that present levels of unemployment are removing the opportunities for many people to acquire a stake in society, and so unemployment is encouraging them to continue occasional, impulsive juvenile delinquency into more frequent, regular career criminality.

(Hudson, 1987: 100)

Unfortunately, sentencers have not responded to increased crime rates by providing opportunities for people to increase their 'stake in society' but have, instead, sent disproportionately more people to prison.

Inequality and punishment

In 1976 a United Nations review of research into economic crises and crime (United Nations, 1976) echoed the classic study of Rusche and Kirchheimer (1939) when it argued that in times of economic crisis societies become less tolerant and punish offenders more harshly. Two reasons were suggested. First, that at such times there is a greater perceived need to regulate and restructure the work-force. Second, that during recession police, sentencing personnel and others in the criminal justice system really do believe that unemployed people are more likely to commit crime. (Such unfavourable stereotyping of the unemployed may well relate to the fact that as inequality increases, the anger which might more appropriately be directed at the government via the ballot box is instead visited directly upon junior police officers, social workers and DHSS officials.)

To investigate the extent to which the posited diminution of official tolerance actually affects criminal justice personnel, Box (1987) reviewed a range of studies about police and sentencers' decision-making. His conclusion was that as the recession bites, each group responds by being tougher on unemployed people – the police because they see them as being more likely to commit crime; sentencers both by meting out harsher sentences *and* by imposing fines that are not realistic in terms of the offender's ability to pay. In fact, a 1984 study by the National Association of Probation Officers (NAPO, 1983, quoted in Box, 1987) revealed that in Nottinghamshire unemployed people constituted about 75 per cent of fine-defaulters. A more recent study by the National Association for the Care and Resettlement of Offenders (NACRO) of unemployment and magistrates' courts found that 'although unemployed offenders were less often fined . . . some moved down the tariff to conditional discharge while others moved up . . . so that at the top end the unemployed went more often into custody'. And even if they were not sentenced directly to imprisonment, 'the unemployed were at greater risk of fine default' (Crow and Simon, 1987: 48). Other people adjudged unable to pay a fine have ended up in prison through failure to complete a non-custodial order which should have been imposed only as an alternative to custody but which in fact had been imposed in place of a monetary penalty. (See NACRO, 1988c for a succinct overview of research on unemployment and fine default.)

Courts and government have been uneasy about the sentencing dilemmas and patterns that have developed in the 1980s. Magistrates have feared that by moving the destitute 'down tariff' they unwittingly imply that poverty licenses crime (Carlen, 1988). Judges have stubbornly refused to use the full range of non-custodial alternatives in the (unsubstantiated) belief that the public is demanding stiffer sentences all the time. The government itself has been alarmed by the expense of an ever-expanding prison-building programme which by mid-1988 had cost almost £1 billion (Home Office, 1988a). In 1988, therefore, proposals for more onerous 'punishments in the community' were put forward as a solution to the government's need to maintain a punitive law-and-order rhetoric while cutting a costly prison population (Home Office, 1988a).

Four sentencing models will now be discussed. The purpose will be to elucidate the elements of penality from which the new proposals have been developed, and to assess their potential for reducing crime without increasing inequality.

Four models of sentencing

1 The general rehabilitation model
   (fitting the punishment to the offender)
2 The justice model
   (making the punishment fit the crime)
3 The community corrections model
   (bringing the pains of imprisonment into the community)
4 The state-obligated rehabilitation model
   (obligation to society – denunciation
   obligation to victim – restitution
   obligation to offender – rehabilitation)

The general rehabilitation model
The general rehabilitation model of sentencing has traditionally been concerned both with punishment of the offender and with crime control. Unlike the classical theory of justice put forward by Beccaria (1963), the general rehabilitative model has always been less committed to making the punishment fit the crime and more concerned with fitting the punishment to the offender – in other words, with an individualized sentencing aimed at

removing (or ameliorating) the conditions presumed to have been part-cause of the criminal behaviour.

Rehabilitationist penology was developed at the beginning of the twentieth century in England and was innovative in incorporating into sentencing a range of extra-legal criteria – medical, social, psychological and psychoanalytical. It reached its zenith with the 1969 *Children and Young Persons' Act* (1969, CYPA) and it was the body of criticism subsequently directed at the working of the CYPA which prepared the way for the decline of the general rehabilitation model in the 1970s and the rise of the justice model thereafter.

After 1969, rehabilitationism (called 'general' in this chapter because it embraces an eclectic mix of psychological, psychoanalytical and positivistic theories of crime) was strongly attacked by critics from both the left and the right. Leftist critics pilloried individualized sentencing on the grounds that it discriminated against working-class youths, black people and young girls perceived as gender-deviant. Right-wing pundits believed that the 1969 CYPA together with the introduction of more alternatives to custody (e.g. suspended sentences, deferred sentences and community services orders) had resulted in too many younger offenders being let off too lightly. Lawyers were concerned that the lack of consistency in (individualized) sentencing was bringing the courts into disrepute; and civil libertarians of all shades of political opinion questioned the right of the state to impose 'treatment' rather than punishment on supposedly responsible citizens. In fact, and as Barbara Hudson (1987) points out, only the criticism of the civil libertarians was directed at an integral feature of rehabilitationist penology. All other criticisms could have been met without abandoning rehabilitationism or even, as Hudson suggests, 'by more and better elements of rehabilitation being incorporated into criminal justice systems' (ibid: 31). Be that as it may, the attack on rehabilitationism united such powerful critiques from diverse political perspectives that the growing calls for a 'return to justice' in penology met with very little resistance. While conservative thinkers hoped that a 'just deserts' model would ensure that criminals would indeed be punished and not 'let off' with a rehabilitative sentence, more liberal proponents argued that the 'net-widening' effects (S. Cohen, 1985) of the preventive treatment of people 'at risk' could best be eliminated by a 'just deserts' model which would punish offenders for what they had done rather than for who they were. Even more importantly, it was contended on all sides that 'just deserts' sentencing would reduce crime. Conservatives claimed that the deterrent effects of *certain punishment* would be greater than those of the individualized (and therefore less certain) sentences of rehabilitation. Liberals, on the other hand, argued that an emphasis on the principles of parsimony in punishment and proportionality of punishment to the crime would reduce the numbers of socially disadvantaged people drawn into the criminal justice system by the misguided policies of rehabilitationism; and that fewer people, therefore, would re-offend as a result of criminal contamination or moral debilitation.

In the rush to renounce rehabilitationism, few supporters of the justice model appeared to suspect that the 1970s attack on welfare in criminal justice might be the thin edge of the wedge as far as welfare provision in general was concerned. In future, it was agreed, the state's role in the punishment of offenders was to be concerned primarily with 'doing justice' (Von Hirsch, 1976) and only secondarily with 'doing good'.

The justice model[1]

The major principles of the justice model of sentencing are desert, equivalence, determinancy and consistency. In 1986 the Home Office's handbook for the courts on the treatment of offenders (Home Office, 1986a) clearly stated that these principles were to be preferred over those of an individualized, rehabilitationist justice. Sentencers were advised that

> a sentence should not normally be justified on merely deterrent or therapeutic grounds – either that the offender will be 'cured' or that others need to be discouraged from similar crimes. It may be that properly reflecting the relative gravity of the offence, and fairness between different offenders, are more important aims in the individual case.
>
> (Home Office, 1986a: 7)

By 1986 however, it had already become apparent that after a decade of sentencing dominated by the justice model, crime and imprisonment rates had increased while the sentences of the courts continued to reflect the inequalities of society at large – that is they still discriminated either against or in favour of certain categories of offenders regardless of the nature of their offences. For instance, while certain women who commit trivial offences still go to prison because they are seen as being bad wives, mothers or daughters (Carlen, 1983b) others found guilty of very serious crimes still receive non-custodial sentences on the grounds that their offences result from abnormal mental or emotional states which can none the less be regarded as *normal for women* (Allen, 1987). Black people also are still being treated differently by the courts – and usually more punitively. For whereas stereotypes of women result in some being made examples of and others being treated leniently, persistently unfavourable discrimination against black people has shown up in innumerable studies. In 1984, for instance, a study by Nottinghamshire Social Services compared the sentencing of black and white defendants in a juvenile court and found that there was 'a greater propensity for those in the black group to receive a custodial outcome' (16.9 per cent as against 9 per cent for the white group': reported in NACRO, 1986a). Two years later the Home Office (1986a) reported that 'the proportion of male black prisoners is about double those in the comparable age groups· in the general population' (NACRO, 1986a); and, furthermore, that even though black prisoners had fewer previous convictions than white prisoners, they were serving on average longer sentences and some of this difference was statistically significant (ibid). Finally, and turning now to income inequality, the sentences of white-collar criminals who commit large tax frauds remain disproportionately lenient when compared with the sentences of poor and unemployed offenders (see Cook, 1988; Chapter 6 of this volume; 1989).

Barbara Hudson, in a passionate and elegant denunciation of the justice model, has explained precisely *why* 'just deserts' sentencing *is* consistently unjust:

> What deserts-based sentencing means . . . is building on class-based definitions of serious crime, ignoring class-differential vulnerability to the acquisition of a 'bad' record and imposing an arbitrary, blind 'fairness' at an advanced stage of the criminal justice process. Ignoring the 'non legal' factors in sentencing means, ignoring the fact that in all its stages, criminal justice is a complex process of negotiation. . . . By modestly demurring that social injustices can be dealt with by the criminal justice system, justice model reformers are building those very injustices into the heart of the system, by privileging the factors they most strongly influence – the nature of the charge faced by a defendant, and the length of the previous criminal record – as the only factors relevant in sentencing.
>
> (Hudson, 1987: 114)

Unless there is an entirely new approach to punishment it is unlikely that implementation of the Home Office's new 'punishment in the community' proposals will either diminish present injustices or decrease crime and imprisonment rates.

The community corrections model

The government's Green Paper *Punishment, Custody and the Community* (Home Office, 1988a) was published in July 1988. Its main proposals were that

1 more offenders convicted of less serious crimes should be 'punished in the community' rather than sent to prison
2 offenders should be made to pay as much as they can to provide financial compensation to their victims
3 to increase public confidence in court orders which leave offenders in the community, the regulations governing community service and probation orders should be strengthened, while day centre projects should offer 'strict and structured regimes' aimed at reducing the offending of young adult offenders
4 'a new sentence might be developed to include
  – compensation to the victim

- community service
- residence at a hostel or other approved place
- prescribed activities at a day centre or elsewhere
- curfew or house arrest;
- tracking an offender's whereabouts;
- other conditions, such as staying away from particular places.'

(Home Office, 1988a: 13)

The penal principles underlying the proposals were clearly stated. Retribution and general deterrence, still the dominant planks of what in effect remained a 'just deserts' policy, were in future to be buttressed by an individualized sentence designed to incapacitate offenders according to their circumstances. There was a new emphasis on reparation both to community and victim.

When an offence is so serious that a financial penalty alone is inadequate, the government considers that the penalty should, where possible, involve these three principles:

- restrictions on the offender's freedom of action – as a punishment
- action to reduce the risk of further offending; and
- reparation to the community and, where possible, compensation to the victim.

(Home Office, 1988a: 2)

Unfortunately, present inequalities of wealth and income will make it impossible to fashion each offender's penalty in accordance with the foregoing principles. Rather, it is likely that as far as non-custodial sentencing is concerned offenders will fall into three main groups. The largest will be comprised of those poorer people who, unable to pay a financial penalty or make compensation to the victim will receive a tough punishment involving close surveillance in the community. In this group will be those whose social circumstances make them least able to cope with any further punishment in the community (punishment, that is, beyond that already inflicted by unemployment and poor to non-existent housing) and who are therefore the least likely to be deterred from crime by stiffer penalties. Another group will contain first-time or other 'not-at-risk of recidivism' offenders who will most probably not reoffend whatever non-custodial penalty is imposed. And a third will consist of better-off 'professional' or 'white-collar' criminals who, having paid a not-too-onerous fine (and maybe compensation) will either be excused 'punishment in the community' altogether, or discover that, within the comfort of their well-off homes and supportive environments, 'punishment in the community' is no punishment at all.[2] Furthermore, if present punitive sentencing practices continue, the tightening-up of the non-custodial alternatives to prison will merely result in sentencers imposing tougher alternatives regardless of the appropriateness or feasibility of the sentence and in offenders then breaching the conditions of unrealistic orders, and ending up in prison anyhow. Non-imprisoned, 'professional' or 'white-collar' criminals, on the other hand, having weighed the light costs of their crime against its very profitable rewards might well conclude that crime *does* pay and have little incentive to change their ways in the future. In short, although there was much to welcome in the government's proposals to reduce the prison population and fashion more socially productive penalties for crime, their implementation would be unlikely to produce the desired reductions in crime and imprisonment rates unless accompanied by other, more radical reforms.

State-obligated rehabilitation
The term 'state-obligated' rehabilitation (though not the model developed here) is taken from F. T. Cullen and K. E. Gilbert (1982) who, in their book *Reaffirming Rehabilitation*, were among the first to warn that a renaissance of the justice model of sentencing might not be the best way to reduce crime and prison populations. Arguing that where rehabilitationism had previously failed it had done so because of the state's lack of commitment to it, they suggested that

> Liberal interest groups should embark on efforts to transform enforced therapy into a programme of state-obligated rehabilitation that takes seriously the betterment of inmates but legitimates neither coercion in the name of treatment nor neglect in the name of justice.
> (Cullen and Gilbert, 1982: 246)

In their programme of liberal reforms Cullen and Gilbert proposed that prison administrators should be obliged to offer treatment to every inmate and that 'all prisoners should be invited to enter a parole contract' whereby they 'agree to complete certain rehabilitation programmes and in exchange are given the exact date on which they will be paroled' (ibid.).

The notion of state-obligated rehabilitation could also be profitably extended to non-custodial penalties, though in the model developed below it would be assumed that, in order to be rehabilitated, offenders would need to be convinced not only that their own behaviour had been reprehensible but also that the state's treatment of them had been *just* – in terms of impact in relation to their *offence* and in terms of sentence feasibility in relation to their *social circumstances*.

A fundamental assumption of state-obligated rehabilitation would posit that as both offender and state might be more or less responsible for the breakdown of social relations which had resulted in crime, both had an obligation (more or less) to take action to reduce the likelihood of similar rupture in future. Such a conception of reciprocal obligation might also displace the punishment/treatment dichotomy:

Imagine for a moment that the court was really concerned only with considering ways in which the living conditions of the accused could be so changed that either he was improved or society was protected from him – and the whole meaning of the term punishment evaporates at once.

(Pashukanis, 1978: 177)

Furthermore, in a model of state-obligated rehabilitation, displacement of questions about the state's right to punish would not be replaced by ones about the state's right to treat. Instead, the state's duty to intervene would be based upon an obligation to do justice (between criminal, victim and state) without increasing inequality. For as Nicola Lacey has recently argued:

if individuals have a fundamental interest in the maintenance and development of a peaceful just society to which they belong and through which many of their interests are realised and indeed constructed, the alleged moral boundaries which dictate that individuals never be used merely as a means to social ends begin to dissolve.

(Lacey, 1988: 172)

Lacey herself recognizes that at present we are nowhere near achieving the ideally just society which she specifies as being preconditional to a just criminal law but concludes that

given the limited extent to which present society is committed to the equal pursuit of the welfare and autonomy of all its citizens, the best option may nonetheless be to support at least some of its practices of punishment, in the absence of any realistic prospect of getting anything better in the near future.

(Lacey, 1988: 196)

Yet it may be that in order to get something better at any time in the future there is a need constantly to call into question the practices of the present.

State-obligated rehabilitation: sentencing principles

The major principles of state-obligated rehabilitation should be

1 that imprisonment is an extreme form of punishment, to be used only in exceptional cases and *never* as back-up to a non-custodial court order;
2 that denunciation, crime-reduction, rehabilitation and reconciliation (between community, offender and victim) should be the major aims of sentencing (see Blom-Cooper, 1988).

3 that punishment should be a primary aim of sentencing only if offender
   and court are agreed that a rehabilitative element would be redundant in
   a particular case;
4 that so long as the state fulfilled its obligation to rehabilitate in a particular
   case the offender could be obliged to engage in any 'feasible' programme
   of rehabilitation or regulation (including, for instance, urine testing of
   drug-takers or electronic monitoring of other offenders). For *no*
   rehabilitative or regulatory programme would be rejected out of hand on
   the grounds of its being an essential violation of civil liberties or on the
   grounds of its being essentially lacking in feasibility. Rather, it would only
   be rejected on the grounds of its non-feasibility in a specific case;
5 that attempts to achieve greater equality of sentence impact should only be
   qualified by the court's recognition that in a specific case an offender's
   circumstances rendered the appropriate degree of punishment non-
   feasible.

Towards state-obligated rehabilitation: suggested sentencing reforms

Sentencing to promote good rather than to impede evil

Implicit in the government's Green Paper *Punishment, Custody and the
Community* (Home Office, 1988a) was the notion that greater use of non-
custodial alternatives to prison is justified only if such alternatives bring
many of the pains of imprisonment into the community. This is a
retrogressive view. The aim of judicial intervention into offenders' lives
should be to help them create living conditions in which they will be more
likely to choose to be lawabiding in the future. Close surveillance, punitive
work schemes, curfews and so on are not necessarily the types of
interventions that will increase all offenders' capacity to change their
behaviour. Indeed a radical approach to rehabilitative sentencing might not
concentrate on the individual offender at all. Rather, it might see
lawbreaking as part and parcel of other social problems. For example,

> excessive numbers of alcohol-related crimes in one area might result
> not only in increased treatment facilities for those with a drink
> problem, but also in intensive programmes designed to educate the
> public about the dangers of alcohol and, in addition, the levies on those
> benefiting from its manufacture and sale might be increased. Or, in a
> different example, excessive youth crime might result in public debate
> about, and investigation and remedy of, the work and leisure
> opportunities for the youth in that area as well as a review of police
> practices in relation to youthful offenders.
>
> (Carlen, 1983a: 214)

When individual sentences *are* being considered, however, the notion that rehabilitation is only for poorer offenders should be abandoned. Every offender should have the chance to say if he or she thinks that there should be an element of rehabilitation in the sentence and in certain cases of recidivism an offender might even be coerced into accepting a rehabilitative order. (For instance, a recidivist business criminal might be required to attend compulsory training sessions on company and/or tax law as a condition of a disqualification being lifted after a period of time. Similar re-educative orders might be made in relation to driving offences, certain sexual offences and other offences based on undesirable behaviour patterns or habits.) No order should be imposed, however, until the court has been assured by the probation service that, in the light of the offender's circumstances, such an order is *feasible*.

Sentence feasibility, social circumstances and the tariff
Although the traditional jurisprudential concern about the difficulties of assessing the impact of the same sentence on offenders in different circumstances continues to be discussed by leading writers on sentencing (e.g. Walker, 1980; Ashworth, 1983) the academic focus upon sentence *impact* has not been matched by a similar focus upon sentence *feasibility*. And there is a difference between the two. Whereas the principle of equality of impact raises questions about the possible inequality of pain or deprivation suffered by different offenders awarded the same punishment, the notion of sentence feasibility raises questions about the likelihood of extremely disadvantaged offenders being able successfully to complete *any* very demanding non-custodial order. Yet though this latter concern has been largely ignored by academic lawyers, it has traditionally been a major concern of the probation service who have been especially enjoined to advise the court as to the feasibility of individual offenders being put on probation or given a community service order. In recent years, however, the punitive 'just deserts' model has so dominated the courts that probation officers fear that if they advise against any available non-custodial order on the grounds of its non-feasibility, their clients will be given a custodial sentence instead. (The numbers of mentally ill and homeless prisoners suggests that their fears are not groundless.) The fundamentally punitive tenor of *Punishment, Custody and the Community* (Home Office, 1988a) is likely to increase those fears. This is ironic, because if some of the proposals in the Green Paper are adopted it will be more important than ever before that courts take seriously the issue of sentence feasibility.

When the Green Paper was published in 1988 it was hailed by certain of the mass media as evidence of a new, 'get tough' approach to offenders. This characterization was rooted in the government's stated determination 'to increase the public's confidence in keeping offenders in the community' (Home Office, 1988a: 2) and the implication that probation services should in future attempt to impress sentencers by making all orders subject to strict and punitive enforcement. (No evidence was presented to support the claim that public and sentencers actually *do* currently lack confidence in the non-custodial alternatives to imprisonment; nor was there discussion as to whether any such lack of confidence might not be more properly attributed to the ignorance and prejudice of the sentencers than to failures on the part of probation.) But it was the eagerness to woo sentencers to non-custodials by presenting them with a mix of orders designed to hurt rather than help that finally over-ruled the Green Paper's reiterated contention that an over-punitive approach won't work – either in terms of reduction of the prison population or in terms of crime control. For although on pages 11 and 12 the Green Paper's authors seemed to be of the opinion that, because of their unenforceability and adverse side-effects, tracking, electronic monitoring, curfews and intermittent custody would be undesirable adjuncts to existing non-custodial penalties, three of these newly mooted forms of surveillance (the exception being electronic monitoring) were mentioned without demurrer on page 13 as possible components of a new non-custodial sentence, and finally reappeared again in the Appendix as part of specimen 'pick 'n' mix' programmes which might well be offered to the courts. In October 1988 the Home Secretary announced that the electronic monitoring of persons on remand before trial would be implemented for an experimental period. If the proposals put forward in the Green Paper were indeed to result in a new order then it should also become mandatory that no persons considered for a non-custodial penalty end up in custody purely because their social circumstances might render such an order impractical. Conversely people who might desperately need the help which the probation service can give should not be denied assistance because the relevant order would also push them 'up tariff'.

The problem of sentence feasibility and social circumstances comes about primarily in two ways. First, because so many people are currently enduring domestic situations fractured by the pains of unemployment, low wages and poor housing. Second, because many areas of the country lack the communal facilities which provide for a decent standard of public life. Thus, while certain offenders might be perfectly willing to attempt compliance with specified non-custodial orders, their probation officers might rightly calculate that, given the tensions and frustrations already existing in their homes, the clients would be unlikely to complete any order involving constant home calls, curfews or house arrest. Similarly, in other cases officers might know that while a lack of child-minding facilities would prevent some parents from doing community service, a dearth of public transport would equally prevent some other clients from getting to and from suitable schemes. Additionally it might also be unrealistic to expect emotionally and mentally damaged recidivist clients to complete a punitive, as opposed to a supportive, order. It would be desirable, therefore, that sentencers be obliged to accept a probation officer's assessment of the non-feasibility of a rigid non-custodial sentence in certain cases, and that, in the cases of offenders bearing multiple social disadvantage, they should attempt to do least harm by making orders that are totally supportive and non-punitive.

A slightly different problem in relation to sentence feasibility arises when a probation officer, though believing that a first or minor offender's social circumstances are such that he or she could benefit from some type of probation assistance, is reluctant to recommend an order that will push the client 'up tariff'. In fact, the whole notion of the 'tariff' in relation to an offender's record – i.e. 'the recommended sentence being the next one higher than the last one served' (Hudson, 1987: 50) – would be abandoned in a reformed system that did not see offenders' records as pushing them inexorably towards imprisonment. (Indeed, it is likely that a radically reformed sentencing programme would abandon the term 'non-custodial alternatives' altogether in favour of some term connoting a more positive form of social regulation – cf. Shaw, 1987b: 14). Certainly in a state-obligated model of rehabilitation it should be the expectation that all offenders would be offered any rehabilitative help that they might need, and that acceptance of it would not disadvantage them if they were to appear in court again in the future. Under the present system it is evident that tariff sentencing involving the ' "when all else has failed" use of imprisonment can . . . be inappropriately punitive to the petty persistent offender, the very offender that most reformers and policy makers think should be kept out of prison' (Hudson, 1987: 50).

Equality of sentence impact [3]

> The principle of equality of impact in sentencing suggests that whilst it is just to impose the same sentence on two equally culpable offenders for two equally grave offences, it is unjust to do so if the two offenders have such differing 'sensibilities' that the sentence would have a significantly different effect on each of them.
>
>   (Ashworth, 1983: 283)

Even on a state-obligated model of corrections, many offenders, as well as being deemed suitable for some kind of rehabilitative element in their sentences, would also be judged as culpable and deserving of punishment. In some cases, moreover, the court would decide that though questions of rehabilitation did not arise, punishment would be necessary both to symbolize the state's abhorrence of the crime and to deter this offender and his/her potential imitators in the future. In such cases it is likely that the fine would remain the most favoured sentencing option and it is in relation to monetary penalties that questions of sentence impact are at their most difficult.

The 1986 edition of *The Sentence of the Court* (Home Office, 1986a) advised sentencers that though they should reduce a fine for an offender of very small means they should not increase it 'because an offender is very affluent'.

> Parliament has provided specifically that a magistrates' court must, in fixing the amount of a fine, 'take into consideration among other things the means of the person on whom the fine is imposed. . . .' Specifying the correct approach, the court has said that 'in principle, the amount of the fine should be determined in relation to the gravity of the offence, and then – and only then – should the offender's means be considered, to decide whether he has the capacity to pay such an amount.' It is therefore clearly not correct sentencing practice to increase the level of a fine beyond what would otherwise be appropriate if that sum is more than the offender can be fairly required to pay within a reasonable time.
>
> (Home Office, 1986a: 25)

It is this approach which has led many people to argue that the relatively small fines imposed on the very rich are derisory rather than denunciatory and deterring. At the same time, it is not an approach (being advisory rather than mandatory) that has prevented sentencers from imposing unrealistically high fines on poorer offenders. Yet, as has already been argued, in order for rehabilitation to have any degree of success in terms of reducing lawbreaking, it is necessary that offenders should see their sentences as being *just* – just, that is, according to the principle that sentences for the same offences should have equal impact on different offenders.

A partial solution to the problem of differential sentence impact on offenders of differing means is to be found in the day fine system of some European countries (See Shaw, Chapter 2 in this volume, for a more detailed discussion of day fines.) This could well be used in England to calculate fines in the cases of all but the very poor and the very rich. Andrew Ashworth (1983) gives a succinct description of the procedures involved.

> For this system the courts must obtain information about the offender's annual income, together with information about his liabilities and any capital he may possess. In general the day fine is assessed at one thousandth of his annual income. Once this calculation has been completed the court can order him to pay so many day fines, the number being calculated according to the seriousness of the case. Thus the two factors, the seriousness of the case and the offender's means, are determined quite independently of each other, and both the number of day fines and the amount of each are announced in court.
>
> (Ashworth, 1983: 288)

But, even if this system were to be introduced into the English courts, there would still be problems in relation to those too poor to pay a fine and those too rich to suffer deprivation as a result of any fine a court would be likely to impose.

According to Peter Young (1987), Sweden has adopted a very realistic approach to petty fine default and it is quite common to remit fines in Sweden:

> Swedish judges argued that the contact an offender has with the court both at the stage of prosecution and at the stage of default is sometimes seen as 'punishment' enough. This was seen to be the case especially for first offenders. Also the opinion was expressed that when the sum of money defaulted on is small then it is simply neither financially nor administratively worthwhile to pursue the offender to the bitter end of imprisonment. [Furthermore] the Swedish judges could not see why their lenient attitude necessarily led to disrespect for the court or the criminal law. Indeed it was forcibly contended that to pursue to the bitter end of imprisonment those who had defaulted on small fines was more liable to create disrespect because it is absurd.
>
> (P. Young, 1987: 287)

Quite so. But what about poverty-stricken offenders who commit more serious offences and rich ones whose wealth often appears to license their crime?

In reality, it is likely that offenders too poor to pay a fine are also those suffering from other social disadvantage and under a system of state-obligated rehabilitation, the court would have a duty to make an order that was at least in part rehabilitative. If in addition the court were to consider it desirable to include an element of retribution in the sentence, a community service order might be imposed with a condition of deferral until such time as the offender was receiving sufficient support to make the order feasible. At the other end of the scale, a progressive (rather than arithmetical) approach to day fines would help ensure that the final sum exacted would hurt the offender despite his or her great wealth (Ashworth, 1983: 291). In the cases of professional and corporate criminals, moreover, deprivation of the profits of crime together with disqualification orders in relation to certain forms of business involvement could be combined with realistically heavy fines to punish and deter. Already-existing 'disabling' measures might also be taken more frequently and more forcefully against not so wealthy white-collar and corporate criminals, and other 'respectable' recidivists such as drunk drivers. (See Levi, Chapter 5 in this volume, for discussion of disqualification orders for fraudsters.) As Ashworth says, 'it will be virtually impossible to achieve equality of impact, but . . . it is fairer to move some distance towards the principle of equal impact than to ignore it altogether' (ibid).

A more democratic approach to sentencing
It has by now become commonplace for penologists to acknowledge that

little can be done to establish a coherent sentencing policy aimed at reducing the prison population until judges and magistrates lose their power to subvert it by sending more and more people to gaol. Equally, it is also widely contended that no constitutional issue concerning the independence of the judiciary would arise merely as a result of their discretion being structured in a more efficient and democratic way. On the contrary, having to negotiate patterns of sentencing with other professionals might help judges shed some of the politico-moral prejudices of their class, prejudices from which their judgments have seldom been free (see Griffith, 1977). As for lay magistrates, the intricacies of sentencing are such that lay persons should not be expected to bear the responsibility without firm guidelines as to practice. To ensure that central policy is supported by the appropriate local facilities, regional and central review committees should be set up to monitor both the sentencing practices of local courts and the local facilities for community corrections. For, if punishment is to be in the community it seems only just that communities should have some say in the types of programmes they are prepared to support.

A Sentencing Council of the type advocated by Andrew Ashworth would go far towards helping sentencers make more informed judgments. The task of such a body, composed of a variety of criminal justice personnel, would be

> to produce . . . sets of declared sentencing ceilings for different grades and types of offence, which have their basis in certain relativities between offences, together with declared principles for use in calculating the precise sentence beneath that ceiling, principles to deal with persistent offenders, multiple offenders, breaches of peace, suspended sentences and so forth.
>
> (Ashworth, 1983: 449)

A state-obligated rehabilitation model might go even further. It might specifically require

1 that prosecutors have the power to waive prosecution and ask for a rehabilitative order when an offender (having admitted guilt) is clearly in need of assistance and when no public good would be served by prosecution (see Carlen, 1983a)
2 that probation officers have the duty to object to the supervision of certain orders on grounds of their non-feasibility and that sentencers be required to justify in open court any over-ruling of a probation objection
3 that *all* sentences be justified in open court and that where a sentencer wishes to make a particular rehabilitative order but can not because of lack of facilities, a record to that effect be made and sent to a regional sentencing review committee.

Summary and conclusions

The major arguments of this chapter have been that

1 The criminal justice system should be used not only to punish criminals but also to redress some social injustices, or, failing that, to ensure that at least its sentencing policies do not increase social inequality.
2 Because fear of punishment is but one factor amongst many more positive ones which result in offenders becoming law-abiding, a purely punitive approach to sentencing (especially one involving imprisonment as the ultimate sanction) will do little to decrease crime and will certainly increase the prison population.

The specific reforms suggested in the latter part of the chapter have not been intended as a blueprint for a radically changed sentencing policy. They have merely been put forward to highlight four of the major impediments to a more rational approach. These impediments are

1 the continuing dominance of the justice model, even in the government's proposals for community-based punishments
2 the reluctance in practice for the courts to elevate sentence feasibility to a major sentencing principle
3 the similar reluctance, in practice, to ensure that the rich pay for their crimes; and the concomitant failure of courts to use to the full the already existing disabling measures that would limit the opportunities of rich business and other 'respectable' criminals to re-offend in future
4 the failure of governments to limit sentencing discretion and make criminal justice more democratic.

Implementation of a state-obligated rehabilitation model of sentencing would not be cheap. On the contrary, in the short term its full implement-ation would most likely cost as much as the present housing and maintenance of a prison population of over 50,000. But with a much reduced prison population, the initial costs of community schemes could be met. Once the initial capital outlay had been made, community projects would be much cheaper to run than the labour-intensive gaols. But there is no *very* cheap way of paying for the problems caused by the positive relationship between crime and inequality. The choice is between continuing to squander millions of pounds on prisons, or developing a rational system of criminal justice which could use the savings ensuing from a heavily reduced prison population to regenerate the communities where, too often, victim and offender continue to live in fear, poverty and isolation long after the sentence of the court has been pronounced.

Notes

1 A thoroughgoing critique of the justice model is to be found in Hudson (1988).
2 See for instance NACRO (1988b: 1) on the way in which electronic monitoring has
   been used abroad:

   The limited evidence available indicates that electronic monitoring is used most
   often for male offenders who have their own home, a telephone and a job; who
   have committed non violent offences; and are able to pay the fees charged for
   the hire of the monitoring equipment and supervision by a probation officer or
   other supervisor.

3 A full discussion of all aspects of equality of sentence impact is to be found in
   Ashworth (1983).

2
Monetary penalties and imprisonment: the realistic alternatives

Stephen Shaw

Introduction

First thing on most mornings, a visitor to one of the magistrates' courts in Central London would witness the following drama being played out.

A succession of homeless people – mostly middle-aged and male – are brought up from the cells to face charges involving public order or drunkenness offences committed the previous evening. After a very brief summary of the facts has been presented, and a plea of guilty recorded, the stipendiary magistrate asks how much money was found on the offender when arrested. Usually it is a matter of a few pounds and an immediate fine of that amount is imposed. If the offender is penniless, the magistrate passes a sentence of one day's imprisonment. However, because a night in the police cells is regarded as being equivalent to a day's imprisonment, the offender steps down from the dock to be released back on to the streets immediately.

It is a swift form of justice. Some thirty or forty such cases may be discharged in little more than an hour. But despite its summary nature, it would not strike the observer as an especially punitive form of justice. Indeed, everyone involved seems to regard the ritual with a certain detachment, even amusement. Equally, no one would pretend that the process serves any social benefit: apart from being allowed to sober up and eat a police breakfast, the offender is offered no further help or treatment. If there is a moral it is that homeless people are better off broke when arrested, because either way they will be broke after they leave court.

Of course, the homeless and rootless petty offender is scarcely typical of the great mass of offenders who are fined after falling foul of the law. Also atypical are the sentences imposed by the stipendiaries which it may be felt demonstrate a rare degree of pragmatism. More generally, the imposition of fines and their relationship to the offender's ability to pay has been fairly characterized by an influential Conservative MP as 'a mixture of bluff or chance' (J. Wheeler, 1980: 10).

Yet despite the fact that the fine is overwhelmingly the most common penalty employed by the English courts, the literature on fines and fine default is not extensive. It is almost as if the everyday nature of the fine (and, for that matter, the relatively undistinguished nature of the crimes for which it is usually imposed) has discouraged the interest of academics and research workers. Even the Home Office, which after all has a material interest in the collection of monetary penalties, has published just one short pamphlet on the subject in the last ten years. Given that in the region of 1.5 million fines are passed by the courts each year, one wonders if there can be any other such commonplace experience which has so escaped the attentions of research. Even the near 20,000 people received into prison each year for fine default are somehow anonymous, lacking the sociological cachet which attaches to housebreakers, armed robbers, or those imprisoned for long periods. The voices of people who are fined are rarely solicited or heard. There seems to be no published study of women fine defaulters, or of young adults who now represent one-quarter of all prison receptions for fine default.

This anonymity and apparent lack of interest is all the more surprising given that the failure to pay a fine remains as one of the principal routes into the prison system. Just under one-in-five of all those received into prison in England and Wales is as a result of fine default. In Scotland, the proportion is an astonishing one-in-two.

It is true, as Table 2.1 shows, that the number of prison receptions for fine default in England and Wales has fallen since 1982 (however, the number remains 20 per cent higher than it was in the mid-1970s). It is true that the average time served in default has more than halved since 1976 with the consequence that the number of defaulters in prison at any one time has fallen rapidly. (Because the average length of stay is only about eleven days, fine defaulters represent only a trivial 1.4 per cent of the total sentenced prison population.) Finally, it is also true that imprisoned fine defaulters are but a tiny fraction – between 1 and 2 per cent – of the total number of people upon whom a fine is imposed. However, in all the debate about the purpose of prison (to reform, to incapacitate, to deter, and so on) one of its main functions seems all too often to be overlooked. The purpose of imprisonment in the case of one-fifth of the people sent there is to 'do something' about fine default.

Fines and fine default

Not only is research into fines extremely rare, the topic seems to receive very little attention from government. There is no mention of fines at all in the Green Paper *Punishment, Custody and the Community* (Home Office,

Table 2.1 Receptions, population and estimated average time spent in custody by fine defaulters at 30 June, 1976–86

	1976	1977	1978	1979	1980[a]	1981	1982	1983	1984	1985	1986
Receptions											
M	15,195	15,184	15,547	16,092	14,976	20,046	23,168	21,920	20,275	19,108	18,084
F	716	856	895	952	962	1,107	1,324	1,321	1,486	1,385	1,075
Total	15,911	16,040	16,442	17,044	15,938	21,153	24,492	23,241	21,761	20,493	19,159
Population											
M	1,046	993	739	761	760	879	871	854	752	540	491
F	26	44	36	30	33	39	38	46	40	23	20
Total	1,072	1,037	775	791	793	918	909	900	792	563	511
Average time served (days)											
M	24.3	23.0	17.2	16.9	17.0	14.5	14.1	14.1	12.9	11.3	10.9
F	14.8	14.5	10.3	11.8	11.8	10.5	11.0	10.1	8.7	8.1	7.9

Source: Home Office, 1987a
Note: [a]Affected by the prison officers' dispute.

1988a) and the keynote statement of the present government's criminal justice policy includes just four sentences on fines amongst its fifty pages. The most significant of these sentences asserts that

> The aim should be to pitch the fine at a realistic level in the light of the offender's personal circumstances and to identify and pursue a defaulter promptly, avoiding resort to imprisonment wherever possible.
>
> (Home Office, 1986c: 24)

However, in essence, this statement simply recapitulates the statutory requirement under Section 35 of Magistrates' Courts Act 1980 to take into consideration 'the means of the person on whom the fine is imposed so far as they appear or are known to the court'. Although not appearing in statutory form, Crown Courts should follow a similar principle which has been set down by the Court of Appeal. Equally, the incantation to avoid 'wherever possible' the use of imprisonment in cases of default has been a feature of successive official reports and inquiries. For example, it will be found almost word-for-word in the report of the May Committee of Inquiry into the UK Prison Services (1979) and in the report of the Advisory Council on the Penal System (1970) entitled *Non-Custodial and Semi-Custodial Penalties*.

What the government will do is remove the *possibility* of imprisonment for fear this would both diminish the amounts which are paid and, by reducing the confidence of the courts, actually imperil the use of the fine as an alternative to custody. This view was supported by a working party established by the National Association for the Care and Resettlement of Offenders at the beginning of the 1980s:

> Little will be achieved simply by saying 'get rid of imprisonment'. The consequences of that would be to undermine the fine and ensure that more people receive immediate sentences of imprisonment.
>
> (NACRO, 1981: 29)

However, it is interesting to note that imprisonment is *not* regarded as the inevitable back-up to the fine at least so far as juveniles (16 and under) are concerned. The law does not permit the imprisonment of juveniles for fine default, instead relying upon other non-custodial sanctions such as the youthful defaulter being ordered to attend an attendance centre on Saturday afternoon.

Before considering enforcement methods in more detail, it should also be noted that despite the retention of imprisonment for default, and despite remaining the most popular sanction of the courts, the use of the fine has in any case been declining substantially in recent years. Between 1977 and 1987 the proportion of offenders convicted of indictable offences who were fined fell by one-quarter.

Few can doubt that this decline in the use of the fine is principally the result of the high levels of unemployment amongst people appearing before the courts. A decade ago, Softley (1978) showed that fines were less frequently imposed upon unemployed offenders compared with those in employment. More recent research in six magistrates' courts has confirmed the tendency – at least for adult men and given similar offending records – for the courts to use fines less frequently for unemployed people than for those who are in work (Crow and Simon, 1987). In turn, this is partly a reflection of the recommendations presented to the court by probation officers in their social inquiry reports. On the whole, Crow and Simon found that those unemployed people who are fined are ordered to pay smaller total amounts (although not by much, especially in connection with motoring cases or those relating to social security fraud), and given longer to pay.

On the other hand, there are suggestions that compensation orders (which these days courts are asked to consider in all instances and which take precedence over fines) are excluded from the courts' assessment of ability to pay. According to Casale and Hillsman, 'the amount of compensation frequently appears to be set without regard for its effect upon the total sum imposed, much less for the relationship of that total to the offender's means' (1986: 21). In practice, 'very often the court was making a gesture at compensation because no significant sum could realistically be paid' (Casale and Hillsman, 1986: 29).

Although it would be difficult to quarrel with the principle of compensation as a way of restoring the *status quo ante*, government proposals in the *Punishment, Custody and the Community* Green Paper for the further extension of compensation payments – perhaps as an element in a new supervision and restriction order – open up the vista of growing numbers of offenders entering into default. While other plans floated in the Green Paper for compensation to be paid direct from the court to the victim and then reclaimed from the offender are obviously beneficial to victims, they still leave open the question of how in practice what may be quite large sums of money can be collected from offenders living on state benefits or low incomes (Home Office, 1988a).

At present, the broad pattern of fine enforcement is as follows. In most courts if an offender falls behind with his or her payments the first stage is to send out a reminder letter. If this fails to elicit a response a means warrant (or occasionally a summons) is issued. At the subsequent means inquiry the court may determine a lower weekly instalment, or in some rare instances may decide to remit the fine entirely. A variety of other options may be considered: a money payment supervision order (MPSO) enforced by the probation service; attachment of earnings whereby the fine is deducted at source by an employer, or the issuing of a distress warrant (seizure of assets to the value of the outstanding sum owed). Only then should the court consider the issuing of a warrant committing the defaulter to prison (a committal which may itself be suspended).

Such debate as there has been about fine enforcement has focused upon the use of MPSOs, attachment of earnings and distraint. Although at first sight each has a part to play in reducing the number of committals to prison, each also has substantial drawbacks.

MPSOs are rarely employed largely because they are considered as otiose by most probation officers who would have to enforce them. Attachment of earnings requires the co-operation of an employer – and therefore brings the offence to the employer's notice with uncertain consequences for the offender – and, by definition, cannot be used for those people reliant upon state benefits. (The idea of an attachment of benefits order – analogous to the direct payment of rent and rates for those on income support – is regularly put forward as a desirable reform by those who do not have to live on benefits themselves. The Department of Social Security is also believed to be opposed to the suggestion of attachment of benefits, presumably for administrative reasons.)

The use of distress warrants – which has been growing in recent years – is perhaps the most controversial of all the enforcement methods. While it has been argued that the notion of 'burly, sinister bailiffs inserting a foot in the door is a myth' (Casale and Hillsman, 1986: 57) in truth very little has been published about the operations of private bailiffs – or, for that matter, of the court enforcement officers or the police themselves who also execute distress warrants. Casale and Hillsman have argued that distraint works 'primarily by threat rather than by the actual seizure or sale of property', although it remains unclear whether the debt is simply transferred elsewhere: within the family or to a money-lender, for example. Moreover, it requires little imagination to see that the enforcement of fines through the threat of carrying off the possessions of an unemployed family leaves a great deal to be desired.

This is particularly the case because research has shown how fine default is frequently but one feature of a multiple debt problem involving HP arrears and rent and fuel bills. Not surprisingly in such a situation the fines are often afforded a lower priority by the defaulter than by the court. Crow and Simon quote one magistrate addressing an unemployed man at a means inquiry: 'You can't mess about with the court. The electricity is not your first priority; you won't be sent to prison for not paying the bill' (1987: 34). Notwithstanding the gulf in experience which such a statement betrays, the part which fine default plays in multiple debt does suggest that some defaulters might benefit from formal debt counselling. However, as one of Moss's interviewees commented: ' "Organise your finances better" we were told. But nothing is nothing however much you shuffle it' (Moss, 1989).

Moss also found evidence that fine defaulters believe the class differences between themselves and the magistracy are an important reason why the rate of payments is set at too high a level:

'The magistrates seem to think if you're on the dole you're a millionaire, but I didn't have a penny to my name. They didn't really listen to what I said.'

'It didn't seem to make any difference what I said. They asked me how much money I brought in and I tried to explain I wasn't sure because of the trouble with the dole. But they said I ought to know and just because I couldn't manage my money wasn't an excuse for theft.'

'I know how much I get and I can guess what the magistrate takes home. . . . My priority is with me, the wife and the kids.'

(Moss, 1989)

For their part, Crow and Simon demonstrated how the whole enforcement process is frequently characterized by muddle, misunderstanding and confusion:

Some defendants had apparently expected a reminder letter from the court before they started paying. Some had not understood papers the court had sent . . . and had ignored them; others had not received papers because of domestic muddles. Sometimes the court records were unclear . . . . Some defendants, after being chased up, had brought money to the fines office only to have it refused because there was now a warrant out for a larger amount. And for many people outstanding previous fines, often for motoring offences, compounded the problems.

(Crow and Simon, 1987: 31)

In other words, most people who fall into default actually have little comprehension of the formal enforcement procedures with which they are faced.

To some degree, this may be because the procedures themselves are unpredictable. Unpublished research carried out by Morgan and Bowles emphasizes the role of court staff in exercising their discretion over the collection of fines. Although the staff of the court's Fines Office cannot reduce the amount owed, they enjoy a wide discretion to lower payment levels, extend payment times, and employ particular enforcement mechanisms. Morgan and Bowles add that 'This is not a question of court staff laxly enforcing the wishes of the judiciary, but rather a question of sentencers explicitly or implicitly delegating to court staff the task of interpreting their wishes' (1981a: 38). In other words, 'the credibility of the fine as a sentence may owe as much to the decisions and resources of court staff as to anything which takes place within the courtroom' (Morgan and Bowles, 1981b: 213).

The research by Morgan and Bowles raises the possibility of using economic incentives to minimize the rate of fine default – for example, by offering discounts for prompt payment. However, this idea seems not to have found favour in government which has instead invested heavily in the computerization of court records which throughout the country until the early 1980s were kept on manual card indices, as they are in the smaller courts even today.

Because of the importance of court staff in the enforcement process, the replacement of inefficient card systems by computers may indeed have played some part in limiting the rise in the rate of fine default. It is not surprising that the extent of voluntary payment and the success of enforcement measures are related to the size of the total fine and the offender's means. However, the significant point is that they are also related to the speed with which a defaulter is identified and the speed of response to non-payment. Broadly speaking, as two of the Home Office's own researchers have pointed out, so long as the defaulter is promptly identified and action is promptly taken, it does not greatly matter what the court does so long as it does something (Softley and Moxon, 1982). Strict conditions of payment tend to reduce the level of default (Softley, 1973) just as severe fines themselves tend to increase it (Softley, 1978).

All of which is not to say that we should not seek to establish a more sensitive approach to fine enforcement. In particular, there would surely be merit in the idea of substituting a community service order for an unpaid fine, as provided by Section 49 of the Criminal Justice Act 1972 but never implemented (Expenditure Committee, 1978). Unfortunately, this proposal has never been welcomed by the probation service – for fear it would result in competition for places on community service schemes with those offenders facing more serious charges and also at risk of custody. In the government's view too, introducing community service in lieu of a committal warrant would add to the complexity of the fine enforcement process and consume probation service resources without appreciably reducing imprisonment in default. However, in March 1988 the Minister of State at the Home Office, John Patten, announced that the government intended to look again at the possibility of implementing Section 49 and would be consulting with interested parties (H.C. Debs, 14 March 1988, c. 419).

Whatever may be the results of this review – and of the desirability of new or additional methods of enforcement – a variety of research studies have now shown that 'courts rarely exhaust the enforcement options open to them before they resort either to the most coercive (and most costly) enforcement device – committal to prison – or to writing off the fine as uncollectable' (Casale and Hillsman, 1986: i). Just as criminologists and government have tended to ignore the fine, so it seems that the courts and their staff have approached the whole issue of enforcement in a manner which is unsystematic in its practice and frequently unjust in its consequences.

The use of imprisonment

In law, the imprisonment of fine defaulters should be confined to cases of 'wilful refusal or culpable neglect' (Magistrates' Courts Act, 1980: Section

88). However, as the following account illustrates, some magistrates also seem to demonstrate their own wilful refusal or culpable neglect in dealing with the poor and disadvantaged people before them:

> Mrs F, a single parent with two children. She was brought to court for failing to pay £202 for failure to possess a TV licence, and not sending her children to school. She had a past history of psychiatric illness. There were no previous offences of dishonesty, and she had not been in custody. She was in receipt of supplementary benefit, and had previously cleared some of the arrears. She stated in court that she thought her husband had been paying the fine. This was not believed. Although the probation officer in court suggested a money payment supervision order, the magistrates sentenced her to 26 days' imprisonment. The children had to be looked after by a friend. She was later brought out of prison after relatives had borrowed money.
>
> (NAPO, 1983)

This account raises two key questions about the use of imprisonment for fine defaulters. First, how far does the use of imprisonment discriminate against the poor? And second, how far does the use (or the threat of the use) of imprisonment actually influence the rate of default? Both questions merit a more detailed exploration.

An investigation for the first issue is made more difficult by the fact that the Home Office does not collate data on the socio-economic status of the prisoners in its charge. Nevertheless, a number of studies have demonstrated that the majority of people imprisoned for fine default are either unemployed or have worked only sporadically as casual labour.

A study carried out in Pentonville Prison, London, in the mid-1970s showed that the majority of defaulters had poor work records and, even at a time of what today appears as a period of low unemployment, only one-third were in full-time jobs (Vennard, 1975). A subsequent study at Pentonville also obtained employment details relating to the previous twelve months. This research found that only 21 per cent of fine defaulters had been in regular employment throughout the year and 55 per cent were living off state benefits supplemented by occasional extra income from casual jobs (Posen, 1976).

The way in which fine defaulters landed up in another overcrowded Victorian local prison – Winson Green in Birmingham – was traced by G. Wilkins (1979). Of twenty-two defaulters interviewed, eight were homeless people who had been imprisoned on the spot for non-payment (that is, expressly punished for their poverty). Wilkins suggested that if offenders most liable to default could be identified it would be more sensible for the courts to impose a different non-financial penalty (for example, probation or community service). More recent research carried out by the Prison Reform Trust at Winson Green and Durham prisons has confirmed that all but a small minority of the imprisoned defaulters were dependent upon state benefits or irregular employment (Moss, 1989).

In their study, Crow and Simon discovered that unemployed offenders were more likely to fall behind with the payment of fines, four times as likely to be the subject of committal warrants, and *four times* more likely to end up in prison (1987: 32). At an aggregate level too, it has been found that there is a relationship between unemployment rates and the use which the local magistrates make of committal to prison for fine default. After reviewing unemployment levels and committal rates for 138 English and Welsh towns, Moxon concluded:

> After allowing for size of court [there is an inverse relationship between the size of the court and its enforcement performance], there remained a strong and statistically significant correlation between committal rates and local unemployment levels.
>
> (Moxon, 1983: 38)

Obviously, we must allow for the necessary weaknesses of aggregate correlations of this kind. Equally, it cannot be immediately assumed that the link between unemployment and committal to prison comes about because jobless defaulters cannot *afford* to pay. As Moxon himself adds, 'the unemployed offender has less to lose by imprisonment (since he has no job) and more to lose by paying (since tight finances mean that payment hurts more)'. It is also important to remember that those fine defaulters who do end up in prison divide into three categories. Those who buy themselves out or are bought out by friends and family. Those who *prefer* to remain in prison, electing a loss of liberty over a financial penalty. And finally those defaulters who would prefer to buy themselves out but simply cannot raise the money. But even when due allowance is made for these caveats (and for the strictly limited nature of the choice made by the unemployed defaulters who elect to remain in prison, or the sacrifices made by the families who buy them out), the overall picture is clear. It is one in which the use of imprisonment for fine default grotesquely discriminates against the already poor and disadvantaged.

The generally upward trend in the proportion of those men who are fined and who are eventually received into prison in default is shown in Table 2.2. As can be seen, an adult male offender who is fined is now approximately twice as likely, and a male young offender three times as likely, to be committed to prison in default as was the case in the mid-1970s. (Figures for the proportionate use of prison for women who are fined do not appear to be collected.) Although, as was noted earlier, the average period of imprisonment in default has fallen sharply, the increasing likelihood of people who are initially fined ending up in prison in default is the grim context for the question of whether imprisonment, or the threat of imprisonment actually affects the rate at which default occurs.

Table 2.2   Imprisonment for fine default, England and Wales 1974–86 (Males only)

Year	Proportion of all males fined received into prison	
	17–21	21 and over
1974	0.7	0.8
1975	0.9	0.9
1976	0.9	1.0
1977	1.0	1.1
1978	1.1	1.1
1979	1.3	1.1
1980[a]	1.1	0.9
1981	1.6	1.3
1982	1.9	1.5
1983	1.8	1.4
1984	2.0	1.4
1985	2.1	1.2
1986	2.2	1.2

Source: Home Office, 1987a
Note: [a]Affected by the prison officers' dispute

On this issue, which is perhaps the most critical of all, evidence collected within the Home Office itself is unambiguous. It is that 'courts which have relatively high committal rates perform neither better nor worse than courts which imprison relatively few defaulters' (Moxon, 1983: 39). In other words, the use of imprisonment is *not* a necessary aid to effective fine collection and enforcement. Moxon's startling research revealed that in the sample period just 9 large courts (out of a total of 650) accounted for 10 per cent of all fines imposed and one-quarter of all committals to prison in default. In contrast, there were 166 small courts accounting for only 6 per cent of all fines but which had *no* recorded committals for default. Moxon hypothesized that bureaucratic pressures explained the recourse to imprisonment amongst the large courts: 'For the hard-pressed court, struggling to keep abreast of its workload, a measure which usually secures payment, and which transfers the burden to other agencies if it does not, has obvious attractions'. It was a simple way of writing off an irrecoverable fine, but a measure which 'has no justification in terms of its overt objectives'.

Viewed in this light, imprisonment for fine default – the exercise of the most severe sanction at the disposal of the state – seems a world removed from the lofty aspirations of the law and the classic functions of the criminal justice system. It has become a mundane, bureaucratic procedure for harassed and overburdened courts: a procedure which almost incidentally condemns 20,000 predominantly poor people to a spell behind bars.

Experience in other jurisdictions

The place of the fine in the sentencing tariff differs from country to country. For example, in West Germany and Austria the fine has statutory priority over short periods of imprisonment, and the same principle (but without statutory backing) applies in Belgium. In France and the Soviet Union – as in Britain – the fine is simply one of a range of 'alternatives to custody', while in Argentina, Italy, Japan and the USA it is not regarded as an alternative to imprisonment at all.

Despite these differences in the way fines are used by the courts, their administration and enforcement raise common issues and problems throughout the world. As a result, most countries allow payment by instalments, provide supervision or community work orders to help offenders to manage their financial affairs better, or deduct payment from wages. For example, in Scotland a system of Fines Officers has been introduced in a number of Sheriffs' Courts. The Fines Officers visit defaulters in their homes to enquire about reasons for non-payment and to see if fine instalments may be adjusted to take account of the ability to pay. Scotland in fact has one of the worst problems of fine default anywhere in the world. Fine defaulters represented 5.9 per cent of the average daily prison population in Scotland in 1986 although this had fallen from a peak of 7.9 per cent at the beginning of the 1980s (H.C. Debs, 8 February 1988, c. 71). Nevertheless, perhaps because average fines in Scotland have risen faster than the rate of inflation, some 7.5 per cent of all people fined in Scotland are eventually received into prison in default, compared with 3.6 per cent in 1981. If an equivalent rate was to apply in England and Wales it would add around 80,000 extra prison receptions each year.

Over nine out of every ten fine defaulters received into a Scottish prison say that they are without jobs, and the average amount outstanding is £134. Taking these two facts together, it is perhaps not surprising that only one-in-four buy themselves out of gaol (Scottish Home and Health Department, 1987). The unlikely figure of the Scottish Secretary, Malcolm Rifkind, has been moved to comment that

> Part of the problem may be that there is poor public awareness of the fact that even a small fine can be an effective and meaningful penalty for an offender who is dependent on state benefits for minimum living essentials.
>
> (Rifkind, 1988)

(See Chapter 3 in this volume, for a more detailed commentary on fine default in Scotland.) In the USA, laws governing the imposition and enforcement of fines are also being revised. Fines are used less frequently in the USA than in Britain and often in *addition* to probation. (It is probation which is the most widely used court order in the USA – in many individual states it may also be combined with community service or as part of a split penalty following a short period of incarceration, as well as with a fine.) The US reforms include fines related to the offenders' earnings, payment by instalments, and restrictions upon the use of imprisonment in default to situations which constitute deliberate refusal to pay (US Department of Justice, 1983).

In some jurisdictions (including those at first sight as different as British Columbia and the Soviet Union), the replacement of fines by imprisonment is absolutely prohibited. In others, fines are used in part as restitution or compensation to victims or as an element in a package involving probation or community service. (Again in the Soviet Union, for example, a deduction is taken from the wages of an offender on a corrective labour scheme. It may be noted that, in general, the countries of the Eastern bloc favour penalties with a nominally 'educative' or 'reformative' function in preference to the fine.)

The manner in which a fixed monetary penalty discriminates against the poor and in favour of the well-to-do is of course the central dilemma of the fine. The most commonly cited way of overcoming this difficulty is by means of what is known as the 'day fine' system. Although often regarded as a Northern European idea, the origins of the day fine can be traced equally to the Brazilian and Portuguese penal codes, under which fines were imposed in multiples of the offenders' daily income (Grebing, n.d.). As a result, day fine systems are as common in Latin America as they are in Europe. Although rejected by countries including France, the Netherlands and Japan, day fines are now in operation in the Scandinavian countries, West Germany, Austria and – wider afield – in Bolivia, Costa Rica, Cuba, El Salvador and Peru (the last named having a system dating back to 1924) (United Nations, 1980; Grebing, n.d.). They are also being introduced in some states in the USA and a pilot scheme along similar lines (although not formally a day fine system) began in two areas of England and Wales during 1988, with two more to follow during 1989.

In Europe, the day fine was initiated in Finland in 1921, followed by Sweden in 1931 and Denmark in 1939 (Thornstedt, 1975). Under the Swedish system the monetary value of the fine is arrived at by multiplying a number between 1 and 120 (or 180 for more than one offence) which represents the gravity of the offence, the number of previous convictions and so on, by a sum of money calculated at one-thousandth of the offender's gross annual income. Additional rules govern allowances for the number of dependants or increases for wealth and savings (NACRO, 1983).

A necessary consequence of the pure day fine is that the monetary value of the fine will be very much greater for the better off as well as very much lower for those who are poor. However, unlike the Swedish system, the West German day fine system (*Tagesbussensystem*) includes minimum and maximum limits for the money value of the fine. As under the Swedish system, this money value is calculated in two stages. The number of day units

(*Tagessätze*) is assessed on the basis of the seriousness of the offence and the degree of culpability on the part of the offender; the value of each day unit is then determined by a consideration of the offender's means. At the beginning of the 1980s the number of day units could range between 5 and 360 and the value of each unit between 2 DM and 10,000 DM. In theory, therefore, a fine for a single offence could be set at any point between 10 DM and 3.6 million DM depending upon its gravity and circumstances and the income of the perpetrator (NACRO, 1981: Appendix IV).

The adoption of prison privatization and electronic tagging from the USA notwithstanding, the criminal justice system in England and Wales has not been noted for its willingness to incorporate ideas from abroad. However, as was briefly mentioned above, the government has now embarked cautiously upon an experiment based upon the imposition of day fines. The first two experimental fine assessment projects began in magistrates' courts in Basingstoke and Bradford in October 1988, with the other two in Swansea and Teesside beginning in January and February 1989. These are not pure day fine systems, indeed it is intended that the courts should have unfettered discretion to take account of all the circumstances in individual cases. However, they do involve the courts obtaining information about the offender's income and outgoings and estimating the amount of 'disposable' income left over. The level of the fine is set in units of a week's 'disposable' income although this is not allowed to exceed the maximum fixed by law for each offence. In other words, there remains a bias in favour of the well-to-do in that they are fined a smaller proportion of their income than are the poor when the maximum penalty fixed by law is less than the multiplicand of their disposable income and the units representing the seriousness of the offence.

Conclusions

The fine is the most uncomplicated penal sanction available to the courts. Of course, where they can be enforced, the objective of compensation payments is to make restitution between offender and victim. However, in most other respects financial penalties have a simple justification: their aim is to punish, no more and no less. (Deterrent effects are sometimes claimed – heavy fines on 'football hooligans' are sometimes rationalized by magistrates on these grounds – but without any evidence being brought to bear.)

In many ways too the fine is the centrepiece of the criminal justice system. Virtually all road traffic offences are dealt with by way of a fine, and it is also imposed in about one-half of all crime cases. Yet in spite of the numerical significance of fine, their use and enforcement is a relatively neglected and unresearched topic. Reviewing what literature there is brings one back time and again to the same half dozen or so studies published in this country during the past twenty years.

From that research emerge three or four common themes. That in setting the level of a fine the courts all too often fail to take account of an offender's means. That enforcement is all too often haphazard and that the prompt identification and pursuit of defaulters is a more critical element in enforcement than the particular measures which are employed. That recourse to imprisonment in default is neither necessary nor inevitable, and manifestly unjust in its consequences. A review of the position in other parts of the world reveals that these are common problems associated with financial penalties in whatever jurisdictions they are imposed.

If fines are to retain their central place in the sentencing structure, the key reform is clearly to ensure that the amount of the fine is systematically related to the offender's ability to pay. The attraction of a day fine system is that it formally punishes offenders equally in terms of the proportion of their income it affects. In addition, the two-stage procedure necessary to set the day fine should also ensure greater consistency on the part of the courts, both between different offenders and between different areas of the country. The exact formulae to be used in a day fine system probably matter less than the fact that 'it forces the courts to consider the economic circumstances of the accused and to account openly for the way in which such consideration has been done' (Thornstedt, 1975: 312). The wealthy pay more, the poor pay less; both pay an equal share of their income.

However, while the implementation of a day fine system in Scandinavia seems to be related to low levels of imprisonment in default, day fines in themselves do not mitigate the requirement for effective enforcement action. Sweden, for example, makes vigorous use of distress warrants and it is the combined effect of day fines and distraint which has reduced imprisonment for fine default to a minimal level. Accordingly there is an important sense in which the present government is right to argue that fines (whether calculated as a day fine or not) are only effective so long as there is an equally effective system of back-up sanctions to enforce them. The government wishes that committal in default should be employed as sparingly as possible. But for its part, the government does not doubt the power which the threat of imprisonment exerts as the ultimate guarantor of the fine.

Those of us who deplore the waste and suffering represented by the incarceration of nearly 20,000 fine defaulters each year should not, in turn, doubt that there are cases of 'wilful refusal' to pay – including a very small minority of motoring offenders about whom it is, on the face of it, difficult to argue that they lack the means to pay. Relating fines to means, offering debt counselling, extending payment periods, reducing the level of the fine or remitting it entirely, may all ultimately fail with that minority of offenders who – for whatever reason – are determined not to respect the demands of the courts. In other words:

Either one disposes from the beginning of alternatives sanctions against certain delinquents resistant to fining and therefore abolishes default imprisonment completely – as was the case in Italy in 1979 through a

decision of the Supreme Constitutional Court and as is envisaged in
Sweden – or it is absolutely necessary to replace default imprisonment
by other effective alternatives, as for instance community service.
Otherwise there is a risk that an effective fight against short-
term imprisonment by means of the fine will remain without success
at all.

(Grebing, n.d.: x)

It has been shown that in general the key to effective fine enforcement is the
speed with which action is taken rather than the specific measures which are
employed. However, if imprisonment is to be abandoned as the ultimate
back-up to the fine, it is inevitable that something must be found to take its
place. For while there may be a case for the greater use of money payment
supervision orders, attachment of earnings (and, some would argue, of
benefits), and even of distress warrants, each of these raises problems of its
own.

Accordingly, there is a strong case for introducing short periods of
community service for fine default in lieu of committal to prison. Indeed, it
is interesting that its deployment as a fine default sanction was in fact a
central element in the thinking of Advisory Council on the Penal System
(1970) in first proposing the introduction of community service as a sentence
of the court. Much less desirable is the use by the courts of community service
and other non-custodial penalties in place of the fine itself when facing
unemployed or impoverished offenders. To do so simply ensures that the
poor are moved more rapidly up the sentencing tariff and is another form of
discrimination in favour of the well-to-do.

This is not to say that there is no case for looking more creatively at the
potential for removing the need to impose fines in certain situations. The
failure to develop diversion to detoxification schemes for drunkenness
offenders only perpetuates the revolving door of court, prison and Salvation
Army hostels which is the lot of homeless and rootless people and with which
this chapter began. It is difficult to think of a more pointless exercise in the
whole criminal justice system than the fining of homeless people with
persistent drink problems. Another example would be the fining of people
caught without a television licence. As the NACRO Working Party on Fine
Default pointed out, the prevalence of this 'crime' (which, for reasons which
lie outside the scope of this contribution, is usually 'committed' by women)
would be greatly reduced if the cost of television licence fees could be
included in the rental charge (NACRO, 1981: para 1.14), or indeed if the
unemployed were exempt entirely.

Doubtless too it would be desirable if the courts could be persuaded to
make greater use of their powers to remit all or part of a fine when a
defaulter's financial circumstances have deteriorated since the fine was first
imposed. And given that the fine is often but one feature of a wider problem
of debt, access to debt counselling services could play some role in enabling

people to prioritize their debts without recourse to borrowing from family members or from loan-sharks.

As they are currently organized, both fines and their enforcement exhibit an institutional bias against the poor. But establishing a fairer system for calculating the money value of fines and a more coherent and sensitive approach to fine enforcement are essential for two reasons in addition to the case which can be made out on egalitarian grounds. First, they would minimize or remove the pressure to find 20,000 extra places each year within the prison system at the annual cost of over £7 million. Second, they hold out some hope of reversing what now appears to be a long-term decline in the use of the fine in criminal cases. That decline would matter less if what takes the place of the fine are penalties which can be set proportionately to the gravity of the offence and the circumstances of the offender in the way it is possible to do with a monetary penalty. Sanctions perhaps based as far as possible on the principles of reparation or restitution. Sadly, it seems more likely that what will increasingly replace the fine are sanctions like tracking, tagging and American-style 'intensive' probation – penalties which exert a further twist to the inflationary penal spiral by transporting elements of custody into the community at large.

3
Punishment, money and a sense of justice

Peter Young

In this chapter I wish to explore a topic largely ignored in criminology and the sociology of punishment. This is the issue of how punishment and money relate to one another. To be more precise, I shall investigate the connections between certain values associated with the institution of judicial punishment and the social relationships and values entailed by money. This is a very broad topic, so to focus discussion, I intend to examine in some depth one point of the legal system where money and punishment are routinely brought together – the use of fines by sentencers in the criminal court. The advantages of this focused approach derive from the place of the fine in the penal system; the fine is the most commonly used of all penal measures and, in this sense, constitutes the very hub of the penal process. It follows from this that a sentence of fine is probably the most common sentencing decision made. Many of these decisions will, of course, be concerned with the great number of minor, regulatory offences that form the bulk of the work of the busiest criminal courts, but this ought not to detract from or diminish their sociological importance. Actual penal practice is mostly made up of 'trivial' business. Moreover, if to this is added the preponderant use of fines in crimes of middling seriousness, together with their frequent use in serious crimes (see Bottoms, 1983; J. Young, 1989), the resulting picture is of a penal system which works predominantly through a cash nexus; for the majority of crimes and offences that appear before the criminal courts, punishment consists of a monetary exchange. Examining how sentencers use fines therefore is apposite; it is at this point that the connections between punishment and money become crystallized and observable.

In what follows I intend to conduct this examination empirically by using data that arises from interviews held with sheriffs in three cities in central Scotland. The interviews were informal and normally tape-recorded.

Although no attempt was made to draw up a representative sample of sheriffs, about 10 per cent of the total number in Scotland participated. The main themes of the interviews were

1 the sheriffs' perceptions of the fine as a punishment
2 the factors involved in determining the actual sum fined for a variety of crimes and offences
3 their views on the common methods of paying fines – that is 'time to pay' and instalment payments.

The culture of punishment and the fine

Before proceeding to the examination of these three themes, it may be helpful to outline the general legal and cultural context within which sheriffs work. The sheriff court is the main criminal court in Scotland. It differs from the magistrates' court in two ways. First, sheriffs are not lay judges; rather they are members of the legal profession who have at least ten years' experience as solicitors or advocates. Sheriffs sit alone in their courts. In terms of sentencing powers, the sheriff court is broadly similar to the magistrates' court. Second, the sheriff court has a much broader civil jurisdiction than the magistrates' court.

There is an important difference between the structure of Scots criminal law and English criminal law. While the latter is predominantly statute based, the former is common law. This means that in Scotland sheriffs have traditionally been seen to have a great deal of discretion in passing sentence in common law crimes and offences.

The Scottish criminal justice system is very often regarded as an extremely punitive one. As is well known, more people per 100,000 of the population are imprisoned in Scotland than in any other European country. Although I cannot go into the reasons for this here, one important factor worthy of mention is the large number of fine defaulters imprisoned in Scotland. Approximately 45 per cent of the annual prison reception population are composed of fine-defaulters and this heightens the relevance of the discussion which is to follow. Whether this sort of evidence can be used in support of this general characterization of the Scots system is debatable; what is relevant in the above, however, is this. There are important senses in which values associated with 'punitiveness' – strict formality, the importance given to proportionality, a stress on the penal system as essentially being about punishment rather than treatment – play a central role in how sheriffs perceive their task and consequently how they sentence. To judge from the interviews, Scots sheriffs have a 'classical' view of the purposes of punishment and of the criminal justice system. By this I mean they subscribe to a set of values that places primary emphasis on rule of law criteria and on seeing the proper way of dealing with crime to be the imposition of punishments, or harms, on offenders broadly proportionate to those caused by the victim. In principle, it is the seriousness of the crime – offence-related criteria – that determine the seriousness of the punishment. Offender-related criteria – facts about the guilty individual – are assigned a subordinate status. For the sheriffs a 'just' penal system is one in which punishment, not treatment or expediency, plays the central role. As shall be shown, this has important implications for how they view the fine. Relative to the other penal measures available to them, the fine is the most straightforwardly justifiable in retributivist/punishment terms. Many of the advantages as well as the problems they see to be connected with the fine have to be understood in this context. It is this belief in the virtues of punishment which gives meaning to the act of fining. Sometimes, as will be seen, the relationship between this general, cultural context and the particular decisions taken within it are harmonious; at other times, however, it is fractured and full of tension.

The interviews

Punishment and the fine

All sheriffs interviewed held two clear conceptions of the nature of the fine; that it is a definite punishment and that it is a flexible penalty.

The first of these conceptions was a dominant theme. Sheriffs argued that the penological objectives of fining were clear: the fine has to be understood as a punishment. For example as one sheriff put it, 'the fine is pure punishment', or again, 'the fine is a punishment, it involves shouldering the recalcitrant into compliance'.

Sheriffs were concerned to distinguish the fine from other available sanctions on these grounds. There was a consensus that, whereas with sanctions like imprisonment other penological objectives like reformation or rehabilitation have to be considered, this is not the case with the fine.

While sheriffs agreed that the fine is a punishment, there was a variety of views on how best to justify it. Generally, in using the term punishment, sheriffs appeared to mean retribution. The fine involves 'a routine prising of injury and damage'. By paying the fine the offender is both punished and the balance of harm restored. Sheriffs were divided on whether the fine can be used as a deterrent. For some, as the 'fine relates primarily to the circumstances of offenders, it is not a general deterrent', while for others,

> the first consideration is denunciation – how bad is it in the public eye. Other things being equal, the fine is determined by this. In so far as the fine is a deterrent then general deterrence is uppermost.

Both the retributivist and deterrence justifications were seen to connect with the priority given to making the amount fined reflect, in principle, the seriousness of the offence. As one sheriff put it,

> subject to statutory and conventional limitations there is a basic equivalence between the extent of damage and the amount of the fine.

The concept of the fine as a punishment was related by sheriffs to two other characteristics. First, all sheriffs saw the fine as a flexible sanction. Second, the emphasis on punishment was connected with the idea that there is a central, voluntary element in the fine.

Sheriffs regard the fine as flexible in two senses. First, it is seen as capable of fulfilling all the objectives of punishment. The fine can be justified as a form of retribution or as a deterrent or as a denunciatory punishment. As one sheriff put it, 'the fine can achieve all the conventional objectives of sentencing'.

Sheriffs thus were aware that it is possible to justify the fine in terms of differing conceptions of punishment, but their main concern is to affirm its straightforward, simple punitiveness. One sheriff commented,

> In 95 per cent of situations the fine is purely punitive, there is no reformative or rehabilitative element.

The fine seems to be favoured by sheriffs precisely because of this. As for them it is a punishment, it appears to satisfy their cultural expectations of what sentencing policy ought to be like. Its apparent ideological purity recommends it to sheriffs. But as well a being ideologically 'pure', it is also flexible. Sheriffs do not *need* to justify it just as retribution; deterrence or denunciation will do as well.

The second sense in which sheriffs perceive the fine as flexible is that it allows them to deal with a wide range of different circumstances and offences. Sheriffs argued that it is possible to use the fine in most situations. One sheriff captured this by contending that 'the fine is a form; its content and its effect is random'. This was seen to be of particular importance as it allows sheriffs to incorporate in the sentence both factors relating to the individual offender and yet maintain consistency with wider objectives. The fine, in other words, is seen by sheriffs as allowing them not only to individuate punishment, but also to keep intact their conception of the wider purpose of the penal system. The actual way in which sheriffs do this is to manipulate either the size of the fine or conditions of payment or both. Moreover, the fine is seen to retain this flexibility after implementation – there is a further possibility of adjustment if the problem of default should arise. This appears to be the reason why sheriffs, while perceiving default procedure, as one sheriff put it, as 'distasteful', still nevertheless are reluctant to lose their control over the process.

The fine is conceived by sheriffs as having a voluntary element – 'the voluntary element in paying fines is crucial'. This aspect of the fine is tied in with their conception of it as 'pure punishment'.

Sheriffs argued that because the fine is paid in money, it provides the offender with the opportunity of behaving in a responsible manner. The financial discipline required by the typical offender – who will be low paid or unemployed – to pay the fine is seen by the sheriffs to have value. In the context of a limited budget, it requires them to give up goods they otherwise would have enjoyed. This both makes the fine hurt and is seen to remind the offenders of their duties as citizens. Sheriffs are aware there is always a choice offenders can make not to pay the fine. The fine allows the opportunity of 'atonement'. It also allows the offender to recognize obligations.

There is another dimension to the general perceptions sheriffs have of the fine. Sheriffs draw a distinction between regulatory offences and 'real crime'. Even those sheriffs who regard this distinction as useless still recognize it. The importance of this distinction is that for some sheriffs it provides the occasion on which their view of the fine as punishment may change. For some sheriffs, regulatory offences, moving traffic and other breaches of statutory provisions, are not really 'fined'. The money paid is more akin to a *post-hoc* tax or licence fee.

For sheriffs who adhere to this view, certain consequences follow. Where it is considered more of a licence fee than a punishment, sheriffs use a formal, but rule of thumb, tariff to set the size of the penalty. So many miles an hour over the speed limit will result automatically in a fine of a certain size. Characteristics of the offender, including income, are seen as relatively unimportant. For example, one sheriff argued that 'television licence fines are not increased to take account of means, because the licence is the same for all'.

Sheriffs who advocate this way of looking at things do not see the 'fine' in these circumstances as punitive. The penalty is not intended to hurt, but merely to mark a form of disapproval. Other sheriffs recognize the distinction but it does not alter their perception of the fine as punishment. As one sheriff put it, 'even in regulatory offences the fine is purely punitive', or another 'there is a division between regulatory offences and real crimes but the fine is a punishment for both'.

Although there is an ambivalence amongst sheriffs on the implications of this distinction, there is a general consensus that many of the regulatory offences that appear before the court ought not to be there. They constitute 'trivial business' and they 'should be removed'.

Furthermore, sheriffs were opposed to the criminal prosecution of social security fraud. They felt that the criminal court was being used to provide 'free diligence' for the Department of Health and Social Security. One argued that the DHSS ought to 'collect its own debts'. Although not all sheriffs agreed with this, it does represent the generally held view. Those sheriffs who were not against such prosecutions *per se* supported them only because to offload them would place them outwith 'the sheriff's humanity'.

The differing views of sheriffs on whether, for regulatory offences, the fine is a licence or a punishment is of significance. For those sheriffs who see fines as licences it means the whole process can be far more automatic than when dealing with 'real crime'. They can place the offender within the tariff without worrying about the consequences of their actions.

As offenders will probably not appear in the court in these cases, the automatic nature of the process is reinforced. Most offenders of this type plead by letter. Invariably it is a guilty plea, perhaps with some attempt to put forward mitigating factors. Sheriffs listen to or read these pleas in mitigation, but this rarely appears to alter the size of the fine.

The organization of court business is another consideration that further reinforces the automatic nature of the process. Pleas by letter are taken at the end of business. Typically the court is empty except for the sheriff, the fiscal, the clerk and the court attendant. The clerk reads the name of the offender and hands the sheriff the complaint, the fiscal briefly indicates the circumstances of the offence, the sheriff makes a decision. The speed with which this is carried out is interrupted only if some 'unusual' claim is made in the letter. In these circumstances, the fiscal may comment, the sheriff may ask a question, but the whole process is still extremely speedy.

For sheriffs who see the fine as punitive there is no necessary conflict between this and processing offences in a routine manner. They can retain their emphasis on punishment and also process statutory offences in the way described above. Their difference with the other sheriffs arises in their not seeing decision-making in this context as administrative in nature. Because statutory offences are the business of the court, decisions on them are justifiable. However, these types of statutory offences are regarded as relatively trivial and thus, in a sense, easy cases with which to deal. As they are easy they can be processed quickly. Although these sheriffs concede that some of the statutory offences should be removed from the court, they argue that while they remain part of the business, they must be dealt with in a punitive manner. These sheriffs thus maintain an emphasis on speed and routine with an emphasis on using the fine in a punitive manner. They perceive there to be no strain or contradiction.

The same sheriffs also use a tariff for statutory offences. Where they may differ is that they are more likely to place the fine at the upper end of the tariff so as to emphasize punitiveness.

Whatever view sheriffs take on this question does not challenge their general conception of the fine as a punishment. The disagreement lies not in how sheriffs perceive the fine, but in how they interpret the nature of the court's business. It is this commonly shared perception of the fine as punitive which underpins their use of it. It serves both to set policy ends and to distinguish the fine from other available sanctions. In the latter sense it categorizes; it establishes principles which demarcate it from other penalties. This general conception of the fine structures how sheriffs use it when faced with particular cases. I will examine this in a number of contexts, beginning with how the fine is perceived in relation to other sanctions.

Flexibility and generality

We established earlier that sheriffs perceive the fine as a flexible sanction that can be used to deal with most circumstances. It can be used to accommodate the particular features of specific cases without this contradicting the perception of it as punitive. Also, in theory the fine can be used for all crimes and offences with the exception only of murder. There exists a group of crimes and offences, however, where the sheriff has to choose between alternatives; either the fine can be used or recourse can be made to the sanction of imprisonment. How do sheriffs deal with these cases?

Much rests upon the place sheriffs give to the fine in relation to other sanctions. Here sheriffs are clear. The sanction which first comes to mind is the fine. A selection of sheriffs' comments make this clear, 'the fine is the first thing to consider', 'the fine is the first and the commonest disposal' and 'the fine is the first option'.

In part this view of the fine rests upon their perception of it as being more flexible than other sanctions, especially prison. The prison incarcerates and thus removes the possibility of doing anything else with the offender. However, this is only part of their argument, for their decision rests also on how they perceive the prison and the fine to relate to one another. There is an interesting difference here. Again sheriffs divide into two groups. The first distinguish sharply between the fine and the prison. Those in the second group see the two as shading into one another.

The opinions of those in the first group are summarized by one sheriff who argued that 'the fine is clearly distinct from imprisonment, it is easily demarcated . . . marginal cases do not exist'.

Sheriffs who distinguish this clearly between fines and imprisonment maintain their argument even in circumstances where they give large fines: 'There is no crossover from large fines to imprisonment'. The reason given is that, as one sheriff put it, 'the link between the fine and imprisonment is completely unnatural'.

Sheriffs in this group see the fine and the prison as serving different functions. Sheriffs perceive the prison as suitable for only the most serious of crimes. It is only the 'wicked' who deserve imprisonment. The 'feckless and women' can be dealt with by a fine. There are other factors which make the use of imprisonment more likely. One sheriff said that 'individual violence or the use of a weapon leads to an increased likelihood of imprisonment'.

Sheriffs regard these as 'special circumstances'. It is only when there is a factor which clearly differentiates an offender or a crime from the normal ones, that prison is to be used. This suggests that for this group of sheriffs, the prison is a residual category in sentencing terms. The normal run of crimes and offences and offenders can be fined, whereas the unusual and serious are more likely to be dealt with by the prison.

For this first group of sheriffs, the use of the fine and the prison rest upon very different criteria. The use of the prison can be justified in only very special circumstances. Consequently the fine occupies a central place. Its flexibility, its 'universal' nature makes it the normal sanction to use for the typical case.

For the other group of sheriffs there is a much closer relationship between the fine and the prison. As a result, they are much more likely to impose a sentence of imprisonment. This, of course, does not mean that they will inevitably do this, because for all sheriffs the fine is the first penalty to be considered.

These sheriffs see the prison and the fine as closely related on practical grounds. The fine and the prison shade into one another when, for example, a particularly high fine is seen to be appropriate. In this situation, the sheriff is likely to sentence to imprisonment if it is thought that there is a high risk of default. As one put it, 'if a fine is unrealistic, then impose a custodial sentence', or again, another sheriff, 'if the sheriff suspected in advance that the fine will be defaulted and the offender go to prison, then he would not have fined in the first place'.

Other sheriffs in this group see the problem rather differently. For them there do not exist clear cut-off points in the use of sanctions. Rather, sanctions are arranged on a scale. As one commented, 'there is a continuum from absolute discharge through to prison'. They place offenders on this continuum by looking at the nature of the offence and the record of the offender:

It is the situation – record, gravity of offence – which determines the fine or imprisonment.

Shading of a fine into imprisonment is very unusual; therefore, the fine is a limited alternative to prison.

The fine and the prison shade into one another; more often, however, prison shades into the fine.

Although there is this internal variation of opinion on the relationship between the fine and the prison, it is clear that for sheriffs as a whole, the fine is the preferred sanction whenever it is possible to use it which is in the vast majority of cases appearing before them. The fine, because it is 'flexible' and 'universal', is the comprehensive sanction. As a result, recourse to the use of imprisonment is rare; the system works in favour of the fine. For sheriffs this is a way of maintaining their belief that the penal system ought to be punitive.

Setting the level of the fine
In this section I wish to explore the way in which sheriffs construct the actual level or size of the fine, how they conclude for a certain sum of money. This question lies at the heart of the fining process.

It is a statutory requirement that in setting the level of a fine the sheriff takes into account the means of the offender. This does not mean that the fine ought to reflect just this, but that it is necessary for the sheriff to consider information about means in making decisions.

The reasoning behind this requirement is to ensure that the fine given has a reasonable likelihood of being paid. To this has been added a further purpose – that of achieving an equality of impact of the fine on offenders. Whether this second objective was a direct intention of the legislature is a debatable point: arguments can run either way. But what is clear is that amongst the sheriffs interviewed and in wider discussions about the fine, it is seen as a desirable objective and one that sentencers ought to take account of in their decision-making.

This statutory requirement can be seen as a legal recognition of the fact that wealth and income are unequally distributed throughout the population. If the fine is to hurt all offenders equally then it must accommodate this wider social inequality. The rich should not be able to buy their way out of the effects of punishment and the poor ought not to suffer unduly simply because they are poor. The problem with this is it seems to allow a possible outcome, that the size of the fine should vary in direct proportion to the means of each offender.

This conclusion has generally been seen as unacceptable by the legislature and the judiciary alike. The objection to it is that it compromises one idea of the nature of justice. How can one have a fair legal system if different offenders suffer differently for the same offence or crime? The radical adjustment of fines to income appears to challenge the maxim that all are equal in the eyes of the law.

There are two different notions of equality at work here. One stresses a formal equality, which is generally taken to mean that punishment should reflect the seriousness of the offence. The other, which has variously been called equality or equivalence of impact, requires punishment to reflect the situation of each offender. A tension exists between these two notions as they pull in opposite directions. Whichever notion is adopted has consequences for the nature of the legal system. If the notion of formal equality before the law is advocated, and if sentencing is based on offence-related criteria alone, then one can anticipate, as a result, a legal system in which there is a high degree of consistency between sentences. On the other hand, if equality of impact is advocated, then there is no premium on consistency of results in sentencing.

The notion of formal equality is deeply embedded in western legal culture. It is one of the main objectives we expect the legal system to achieve. Yet, equality of impact reflects values of a wider, but as desirable, sort. Both notions of equality are instantiated in the law but in different ways. The notion of formal equality is central to legal culture but is not explicitly stated in statutes relating to the fine. Rather, it is a general presumption that may be said to 'lie in the mind' of all legal actors. The notion of equality of impact in contrast can be seen to have explicit statutory statement: it is a formal legal rule. Admittedly the statute does not absolutely require the sentencer to adjust the fine to means – it simply requires him to take them into account – but this intention can be 'read' in. Because these two notions of equality pull in different directions, there exists a tension between them.

This tension is acute at the point of decision on how much to fine an offender. Do sheriffs fine on the basis of offence-related or means-related criteria? The evidence from the interviews describes a complex situation. The general inclination of the sheriffs is to put offence-related criteria first. Their first consideration is the seriousness of the offence; it is part of their general punitive stance. One sheriff put it this way,

> Strict proportionality of the fine to income would contradict proportionality to offence. Therefore, there are limits to proportionality; in effect the offence comes first.

All but a few sheriffs argued this way. Consideration of income, for most sheriffs, takes a second or third place. The order in which the factors are considered can be described in this way: (1) offence; (2) record of offender; and (3) income and family circumstances. Different sheriffs may substitute between (2) and (3), but nearly all of them placed offence-related criteria first. Those sheriffs who differ do not necessarily place income first. Rather, they claim to treat all factors simultaneously. Two examples illustrate this point:

> The offender's means are a factor, alongside the offence, record and so on.

and

> It [the fine] is influenced by: income, record, ability to pay, nature of offence – in no particular order.

No sheriff placed income-related criteria as the first consideration. Seemingly, all sheriffs thus work on a principle of formal equality and then try to accommodate for equality of impact.

However, the position is more complex than this. The actual amount of money fined reflects also what sheriffs call the 'going rate'. By this, they mean not only the amount of money it is conventional to fine for a particular offence or crime, but also a convention on how much the typical offender that appears before them can reasonably be expected to afford, regardless of the seriousness of the offence. The 'going-rate' in this second sense, is not established by reference to the income of *particular* offenders. Rather, it is set by the general economic climate.

For example,

> the magnitude of the fine is in proportion to the economic climate.

> The fine is in proportion to generally limited means. It is restricted in a non-affluent society.

The 'going-rate' sets a very real limit on how far the fine can reflect seriousness of offence. To go beyond the 'going-rate' could well end up with the offender defaulting and being imprisoned. As we pointed out above, sheriffs are extremely reluctant to see this happen. This constrains their action considerably. One consequence of it is that offence-related criteria in fact operate within a wider appreciation of criteria related to income. These latter criteria do not bear down upon the individual offender but upon the means available to the common mass. Former equality thus operates within a wider conception of equality of impact.

In the light of this, do sheriffs adjust the fine to reflect the means of the individual offender? Sheriffs do adjust the fine, but within very narrow limits. Any movement upwards or downwards is limited by the stress on formal equality and by the impact of the general 'going-rate'. Sheriffs express a reluctance to lower the size of the fine too much as they consider the 'going-rate' argues for low fines anyway. Also, to lower the fine for offender X as against offender Y could well contradict the emphasis on formal equality. Hence, adjustment of fines to low income is bounded mostly by substantive considerations.

Different sheriffs operate these rules so as to produce different outcomes. Some sheriffs claim that they are more likely to increase fines in proportion to income because the norm is so low that they feel they could go no lower. For example,

> It is more usual to increase the fine in proportion to means than to decrease from the norm because the norm is rooted in low income. The tariff is based upon unemployment.

Another sheriff argued a similar case:

> The scope for increasing the fine according to ability to pay is limited because most offenders are poor anyway.

Another sheriff completed the argument by commenting:

> Any increase is not strictly proportionate, more of a gesture.

Other sheriffs observed that they adjusted all fines for income, but recognized, at the same time, the limits described above.

There were other considerations mentioned which affect whether the fine is adjusted for income. For example, it appears to be more common to reduce for income in the case of the less serious of the common law crimes, such as breach of the peace. For more serious crimes, however, the fine is likely to be increased if the sheriff concludes that the offender is able to afford it. By doing this, they emphasize the punitive nature of the sanction.

The actual figure of the fine is calculated by a rule of thumb. Sheriffs combine a knowledge of the typical fine given for the offence or crime, with a figure that represents an adjustment to the average net weekly income of the offender. The average net weekly income forms the norm which can be adjusted for offence-related criteria or other relevant criteria such as whether the offender is married and if there are children. Information about income is gained by asking the offender or the offender's agent in the court.

In conclusion, it seems that the criteria used to determine the size of the fine are centred on income-related criteria. Although sheriffs place offence-related criteria first, the practical realities of constructing the fine force sheriffs to resort to income-related criteria.

The central role monetary considerations play in setting the level of the fine creates considerable practical problems for the sheriff. One sheriff expressed this succinctly. He argued that a penal system which depends upon money will inevitably run into crises when there is less money about. Increasing unemployment means that the average income of the typical offender is continually falling. Either sheriffs lower fines in recognition of this, or they must contemplate sending an increasing number of offenders to prison for default. Their only other alternative is to use the fine less, but this is a limited option. The sheriffs interviewed recognized this, and were not sanguine about the possibilities of solving it.

Setting instalments: time to pay

With the exception of very special circumstances, all offenders must be given time to pay their fines. The sheriff also has the option of allowing payment of the fine by instalments. Either the offender requests this facility or the sheriff can offer it. Instalment payments are now a very common way of administering the fine, not least because this helps to minimize the possibility of default. However, sheriffs are ambivalent about instalments. Some argue that instalments change the nature of the fine. Either they lower the fine's punitive impact or they transmute the fine into a far more serious punishment than it was intended to be by extending it over time. There is a further dimension to the problem. All sheriffs are conscious that instalments make income-related criteria central to the fining process. This further threatens the importance of offence-related criteria. A concern with money appears to displace a proper emphasis on punishment.

The majority of sheriffs accept the idea that payment by instalments is a necessary feature of the fine. They appear to resent it, however, sensing the passing of a definite price paid and they also regret the development of, as one sheriff put it, a 'sin now pay later' society, or 'crime on the HP'. But they invariably accept it as the only practical way in which offenders can pay their fines. The following comment is illuminating:

> I have no objection to instalments but their use does alter the nature of the fine. For example, it used to be the case that one 'paid up or else' but now it is seen as an 'extended hire purchase penalty'.

Sheriffs respond to this perception in a number of ways. There are those who see it as offering a positive opportunity to impress monetary discipline upon offenders.

> Instalments do have a positive advantage because they remind the offender each week of his punishment.

The constant reminder and persistent bother of regular payments is seen to serve a purpose: it extends the control of the court over an offender's life-style.

> Bother is the key to the fine, longevity of instalments is the punishment . . . two to three years is no problem.

and

> Instalments can be a positive advantage, because of the reminder element.

It consistently limits the standard of living and ensures that a sacrifice must be made. This achieves the punitive purposes sheriffs hold to and also 'disciplines' offenders by influencing how they manage their budget.

It is these purported 'benefits' of instalments which lead other sheriffs to question their use. They argue that the extended control over an offender's life-style is unwarranted for a number of reasons. For example, sheriffs see it as a good principle that punishment should have an end rather than be protracted indefinitely.

> Law implies that proceedings should not go on for too long. Decision-making and the disposal should be decisive, too long is too onerous.

and

> The fine should have the possibility of being paid in a reasonable time, if not then either lower the fine or incarcerate in the first place.

Similarly these sheriffs worry that the regular payment of instalments, by becoming routine, tends to dilute the original sanction. By splitting it into a number of easy payments, instalments appear to contradict the punitive aspect of the fine. As one sheriff put it, 'The purpose of the fine is not to take their money away gradually, the aim is to pay the fine. Otherwise imprisonment is more suitable'. This is seen as inconsistent both with the 'voluntary' element inherent in the fine and also with the idea that the fine ought to hurt. In order to limit this, most sheriffs have a definite period in mind over which repayment is allowed. Typically the maximum is set at one year.

There are other sheriffs who do not feel so constrained and may allow payment over a longer period, even up to three years. These sheriffs are in a minority and tend to be those who argue for the disciplinary 'benefits' of instalments.

There is another general worry sheriffs have about instalments. This concerns the persistent offender who collects fines on a regular basis. The use of long periods of repayment is said to create a situation whereby fines tend to run into each other. Some offenders end up paying many fines over long periods and are incarcerated for default. For the majority of sheriffs this justified the maximum instalment period of one year; as one commented,

> There has to be an end, not least because there is a problem with fines running into each other because offenders go on accumulating fines.

The general worries sheriffs express about instalments are reflected also in the process by which they actually set the rate of repayment. It is here that the tension between offence-related and income-related criteria reappears. The problem sheriffs face is to set a rate of repayment which is realistically related to income without this either softening or increasing the punitive nature of the fine. They manipulate the situation in a variety of ways. Sheriffs may set a relatively low fine but impose quite severe conditions on instalment payments. In doing this they can adjust the fine to income, yet still make it 'hurt' the offender. Each instalment is set so as to maximize its impact on the offender, but as the overall fine is relatively low, there is little chance that default will occur. If it should arise, the instalments can be eased. Sheriffs who manipulate in this way tend to believe that the 'real' punitive effect on fines lies in the weekly instalment rather than the aggregate amount. For example, 'the use of instalments can increase the magnitude of the fine', and 'the instalment should hurt, especially if the offence is serious'.

Typically these sheriffs are keen to see that fines are paid sooner rather than later. They tend thus to set both high instalments and limited time to pay. The one-year maximum is never exceeded and is really only used for those who default.

By setting a relatively low fine but imposing strict conditions on repayment these sheriffs see themselves as combining offence-related and income-related criteria. The low fine reflects income, and the limited repayment period and high instalments reflect offence criteria. This allows them to stress the punitive nature of the fine. Also the financial discipline imposed on the offender is seen to reassert the voluntary element sheriffs see as important in fining. This combination of variables is seen to force offenders to recognize their obligations by paying a proper price for the harm they have done.

Other sheriffs pursue these same broad ends by reversing the order. They set a high initial fine and then adjust it to income via instalments. One sheriff explained it this way:

The aggregate amount of the fine must have some dramatic impact because weekly instalment must be affordable and, therefore, reasonably easy to pay off.

They see this as marrying both sets of criteria. The size of the fine reflects offence criteria, while instalments reflect income criteria. These sheriffs are more likely also to extend the period of repayment and to welcome the disciplinary effects of instalments. This leads them also into approving, as their other colleagues tend not to, the introduction of fine enforcement officers. For example, 'fine enforcement officers are approved because they remind, irritate and bother offenders'.

There is another aspect to setting instalments which is of considerable sociological importance. Both sets of sheriffs, but especially the second, engage in a form of negotiation with offenders in the court over the size of the instalment. If income is relevant to the instalment then some information about means must be gained. Sheriffs gain it by asking the offender on the spot. This is followed by a short negotiation between the sheriff and the offender over the actual size of the instalment.

The negotiation takes two forms. In one, the sheriff ascertains weekly means and then sets both a time limit for repayment and the size of the instalment. The offender responds by saying he cannot afford the instalment and the time period for repayment is too short. The sheriff *may* in turn respond by asking the offender how much can be afforded. The offender replies and then the sheriff may lower the instalment, or extend the time period. In the other, the reverse happens. The sheriff asks the offender how much can be afforded and the offender responds – for example £2 per week. The sheriff then, if it is thought the offender can afford more, sets the instalment at, say, £3 or £4 per week.

Sheriffs, if they entertain this at all, seem predisposed to lower instalments more readily in statutory offences and for the young or the 'feckless' offender. If the offender is employed and has few or limited commitments, then the negotiation probably will not take place at all. For this latter group of offenders, adjustments are more likely to be made only if default occurs.

This negotiation is extremely one-sided. Sheriffs are not obliged to listen at all. However, when it does occur, and it is quite common, then it is of considerable interest. It differentiates the fine from other sanctions. One cannot imagine such negotiations taking place over a sentence of imprisonment. A sentence of imprisonment has an all or nothing quality about it. Offenders cannot say that they cannot 'afford' to go to prison for six months but would prefer three.

This process of negotiation is unique to the fine. Again, it is an example of the extreme flexibility of the fine as a sanction.

Discussion and analysis

The analysis of the sheriff interviews provides abundant evidence in support of a claim made earlier – that the primary end sought after by sheriffs in sentencing is the achievement of justice through the use of punishments. This may seem an obvious or even idle comment to make, but it has great import. It shows that sheriffs perceive sentencing to be above all else a moral issue. While they have to come to terms with the formal legal requirements of their office and of the sanctions they impose, they seek after a wider, substantive end, justice. For them a just system is one which endeavours to balance the illegal wrongs done by criminals by an equivalent but legitimate harm inflicted on the guilty party. Justice and punishment are closely connected; the one is the means to the achievement of the other.

The place of the fine in this is central. It is the sanction they regard as most easily justifiable in most circumstances in terms of their classical views of the nature of punishment and also the one most flexible administratively. Partly because of the type of offender and offence that appears before them, partly because of the constraints placed on them by convention and statute, other sanctions lack conceptual and ideological purity. Other sanctions are 'contaminated' by values (such as treatment) which compromise their use with the result that they cannot carry the message of punishment the sheriffs wish most to convey. Using the fine on the other hand can carry this message. It allows them to achieve their desired ends with integrity and coherence.

The fine is the most used sanction because it exists at that point at which ideology converges with administration. Sheriffs approach sentencing in the moral way described, but at the same time their actions are limited and constrained. They are charged with a dual mandate; achieve justice but do so in the most expedient fashion. In the vast majority of cases they deal with, the fine is the only sanction it is practically possible to use. The great bulk of their criminal work is to do with the trivial and the routine and to use any sanction other than the fine is either ruled out by statute or existing practice. In the more serious, but still relatively minor, crimes they have a discretion to use other sanctions, but to do so can be both troublesome, as it prolongs the process and so slows down the system, and also brings them into contact with a set of values about which, at best, they are ambivalent. The use of the fine in such circumstances meshes the moral message with the administrative reality. Punishment is achieved but at some cost.

One of the costs the sheriffs recognize is that the use of the fine results in a penal system which in many ways is not as punitive as they would like. They perceive the fine as a punishment, but a 'light' one. If the use of imprisonment did not give rise to the administrative and conceptual complications that it is seen to, then, I was left with the impression that in many circumstances it would have been preferred. Conceiving of the fine as a punishment is not inconsistent with a perception of the prison as a more serious one. Their 'argument' is not with the scale of values by which seriousness is measured, but with the constraints placed on their actions by the factors I have mentioned. If these factors were to be removed – for example, if the sheriffs were High Court judges dealing with serious crimes – then I was left with little doubt that they would use the prison. However, they are not and their views on what it is practically possible to do alter accordingly. That this results in a penal system less punitive than one they would ideally like is a cost they have to bear.

There is another cost arising from the use of the fine with which they have to live. This is the potentially corrosive effect the fine can have on achieving equality in punishment. As we observed, the need to take into account the means of the offender in setting the level of the fine causes a dramatic shift in favour of offender-related criteria at the expense of offence-related ones. This is a problem for the sheriffs because, as was explained, their basic inclination is to set the level of the fine by offence-related criteria and they hold to this because of their underlying retributivism. The statutory requirement to take into account offenders' income considerably blunts, however, the realization of this type of proportionality in order to achieve a second type that is the degree of pain caused by the deprivation of a commodity like money. Proportionality can thus pull in two directions: one towards the achievement of formal equality related to seriousness of crime and the other related to the income characteristics of the offender. In our analysis of the interviews we showed how sheriffs manipulate 'time to pay' and 'instalment' patterns in order to relax the tension that can arise from the desire to achieve the former and the requirement to achieve the latter.

One very concrete way this statutory requirement to take into account offenders' means affects the making of decisions can be seen in the relationship that exists between the economic resources of the offender and the 'going rate' of fines. There is a relationship between the income of the 'typical' offender who appears before the court and the constraints this places upon the decision-making of the sheriff. In order both to minimize the possibility of default and for the reasons described above, the sheriff will adjust the fine to income. But the only income many of the offenders have will be social security payments of one type or another. Sheriffs were aware that any fine imposed on such individuals is a major commitment, not only to the individuals concerned but also to their families in many cases. Social security payments are so designed as to leave little or no disposable income. How do sheriffs act in these circumstances? As was pointed out earlier, sheriffs are more likely to lower fines than raise them, but they see reasons of justice which put limits on the degree to which they can do this. Offence-related criteria cannot be ignored altogether. Nevertheless they must and do adjust fines downwards in recognition of the fact that the individual is on social security. The end product of this process is that over a period, the going rate of fines in real terms is dragged down. The level of social security payments becomes reflected in the going rate; it has a generally depressing effect.

There is another more general dimension to the effect money has upon the mechanisms of decision-making which also has implications for the achievement of justice as it is understood by sheriffs. This centres on the relationships between the nature of the 'commodity', the deprivation of which constitutes the punishment, and the notion of formal equality which, as we have seen, forms an important part of the sheriff's notion of justice. My point is that because the fine is paid in money it introduces an element into decision-making that threatens to put in question the degree to which formal equality of sentence between offenders can be achieved. To explain this I shall contrast what I call the 'original position' of a sentencer when passing a sentence of imprisonment as compared to the original position when passing a sentence of fine.

It can be argued that an individual's right to liberty is seen, in modern, liberal, democratic societies, to be near an absolute as anything can be, subject only to certain important, but minimal, tests such as mental competence. This has a direct bearing on the process of sentencing somebody to imprisonment. The sentencer can presume each individual is in a formally equal position as each, as it were, 'possesses' the same 'quantum' of freedom. The original position thus is one of the formal equality of all subjects. Because of the way we regard liberty the sentencer is acting reasonably in making this assumption. Of course, at some later stage, the sentencer may wish to vary the sentences of imprisonment as between two individuals, but this decision will be made on factors that are secondary and extrinsic to the primary original position. For example, the sentencer may regard one individual to be more culpable than another, or there may be specific factors connected with an individual that allow the sentence to be individuated. Hence, although the final product of the decision-making process – the sentence – may vary between two individuals (presuming they have committed the same crime) it began with a presumption of formal equality.

The original position in sentences to the fine is very different. A sentencer who presumed any two individuals are in a formal equal position as regards that commodity – money – they are about to be deprived of would be considered to be acting unreasonably. It is acknowledged that money is a commodity each of us has in varying degrees. This, presumably, is one reason why sentencers are instructed to take into account offenders' means when levying the fine. The original position is thus the reverse of that which can be presumed in the use of imprisonment. It is one in which the only way of treating individuals equivalently is to presume they are in an unequal position as regards that the loss of which will be the punishment.

None of this should be seen as saying that the idea of formal equality as a component of justice is absent from the process of fining. The exercise of sentencing is carried out within a framework in which formal equality is a major consideration. What the above shows is, first, that different sanctions have a different relationship to the achievement of justice and, second, that money acts as an independent factor.

There is an irony here. As has been shown, sheriffs regard the fine as the sanction, relative to other available ones, which most clearly and easily carried the message of punishment. They see it as the only true punishment they have left. However, this sanction has an inherent potential to corrode the very purposes after which they seek. It drags down the going-rate in the way described; it requires them to reason from a position which collides with their overall general aims. As a result, 'punishment, justice and money' can be seen to pull in different directions: to exist in a state of permanent tension.

Conclusion

This chapter has examined one point of the legal system where punishment and money are connected and noted some of the tensions that arise therein. Its focus has been purposely narrow. It ought to be clear, however, that the themes explored here raise broader questions about the relationship between punishment and money.

One such question concerns the wider cultural context and meaning of punishment and money as general sociological phenomena. In many ways punishment and money have very different cultural resonances and connotations. Punishment, following Durkheim (1984) symbolizes the emotive; it is a 'passionate' response to perceived wrong-doing and thus appears as a collective representation of those values and mores at the heart of group life. Consequently many of the rituals surrounding punishment, the signs by which we recognize it, are sacred; from a Durkheimian point of view the idea of a profane punishment is a contradiction in terms. By contrast, money and the social relationship within which it is instantiated, touch upon a different set of cultural values. Although it too has symbolic force, the message conveyed is different in tone. As Simmel (1978) argued, money represents that which is destructive of group life; it evokes the material and the selfish – those forces of avarice that threaten to rob us of meaning and of the grace of community. It brings disenchantment by forcing us to exchange (for a certain price) even those things we hold most dear.

The idea of money as a punishment sits somewhat uneasily with respect to these broader forces. At one level, as I have sought to explain, it is the most common penal sanction. But at another level, there exists a profound dissociation; in important ways money does not fulfil general cultural expectation of what punishment ought to be like. There exists what I call in a different place (P. Young, 1989) a 'cultural estrangement' of punishment and money which can be seen also in the workings of the criminal court. Consider, for example, why there is a general reluctance to use fines in cases of rape. Although it is legally possible to use the fine as a punishment for rape, who dares fine the rapist?

There exist a small but vitally important number of such crimes in which the use of money is limited. These are normally crimes which are seen to affect central aspects of our notion of 'personhood'; there are some things which are still placed beyond the reach of monetary exchange. Although small in number, they have an immense symbolic significance as they colour general cultural views of the nature of punishment and of its legitimacy. In these cases it is the prison that is seen as the proper punishment; penal values shift from a focus on resources to a focus on the immediacy of the body and the person and attack that aspect of it which is most highly valued – its autonomy, its freedom.

It is beyond the scope of this essay to explore these wider questions in any depth. But they are relevant. Even this very brief consideration of them shows that relationships between punishment and money are complex. At one level of the criminal justice system they are estranged, but at another level they are clearly brought together as is demonstrated by the wide spread reliance on the fine. It is the belief in punishment as the proper, just, purpose of the penal system that makes this possible. My analysis of how a group of sentencers reason, and how they justify their use of fines has sought to show at least this.

4

Fines for women:
paradoxes and paradigms

Hilary Allen

Let the various offences against the Wireless Telegraphy Act (which relates
to the licensing of televisions and has previously been little celebrated in
criminology) be accorded a brief moment of distinction. Of all the crimes
which yield enough convictions of both sexes to allow statistical comparison
of sentencing, it is only in this one category that the pattern runs contrary to
the trends discussed in this chapter.[1] The countertrend is barely perceptible,
and I offer no separate analysis: but at least let all watchers of unlicensed
televisions be forewarned that my discussion may exclude them.

This chapter offers two related analyses of sexual discrepancies in the use
of fines. The first section examines the statistical evidence, and demonstrates
that beneath the apparent parity of the figures, there are important sexual
differences, both in the kinds of offences which typically attract fines, and in
the overall balance between fines and other disposals. The second section
analyses some of the processes of judicial reasoning which underpin these
statistical discrepancies. It describes characteristic differences in the considerations influencing the outcome of male and female cases, and identifies a
variety of manoeuvres through which female offenders tend to be steered
either downwards from fines into low-tariff sentences, upward from fines
into probation, or downward from high-tariff sentences and back into fines.
The objective of these analyses is not simply to expose the fact of sexual
discrepancy, or to demand that it be remedied. Instead, the objective is to
demonstrate, using these female cases as illustration, that there are
intelligible alternatives to some of the more unthinkingly punitive practices
of current sentencing. Like some of the female cases examined here, many
cases which are currently dealt with by fines could easily be dealt with by
low-tariff sentences. Equally these cases illustrate the use of probation as an
alternative to financial penalties, and the use of financial penalties as an

alternative to imprisonment. The various issues raised by these options are explored in the final section.

The statistical paradox: parity but inequity

Fines are overwhelmingly the commonest disposal for both male and female offenders, and account for almost exactly the same proportion of all disposals for either sex. Overall, fines account for 84 per cent of all male disposals, and 85 per cent of all female ones. The similarity of these figures is in decided contrast to the disparity in the figures for other types of disposal. The rate of high-tariff sentences (community service and suspended or immediate imprisonment) is three times greater for males than for females. Probation, on the other hand, is almost twice as common for female cases, and the same is also true of the 'low-tariff' disposals – binding over, and conditional or absolute discharge. In the face of such obvious disparities in the other disposals, the figures for fines invite a degree of complacence: it is tempting to regard the numerical parity as indicating an absence of sexual bias, and to see the popularity of fines as effectively a 'levelling' factor in the overall distribution.

Examined more closely, however, the situation is far less simple. Most obviously, there are major sex differences in the use of fines for different categories of offence. In the majority of categories, the balance is against the imposition of fines upon women: in cases of violence against the person, for example, fines are imposed in 40 per cent of male cases but only 25 per cent of female ones. In a few instances, however, the reverse situation applies. The most striking of these is that of indictable motoring offences, in which 73 per cent of female cases result in fines, as compared to only 53 per cent of male cases. Viewed in isolation, such differences seem arbitrary. It is only when one locates them within the *overall* distribution of disposals that the underlying pattern becomes clear.

Table 4.1 shows the overall distribution of disposals for each of the categories of offence which have sufficient convictions of both males and females to allow statistical comparisons.[2] The categories are arranged in order of the proportion of low-tariff sentences, taking the female cases as the reference point. Those categories which attract the largest proportion of low-tariff sentences appear high on the list, while those with smaller proportions of low-tariff sentences appear lower down.

Table 4.1 illustrates some quite general points about the distribution of sentences, as well as some specific ones about sex differences and fines. In the first place, and irrespective of gender, it is clearly not always the most trivial and minor offences which attract the highest proportion of low-tariff sentences. An offender convicted of a dog-licence offence, or of cycling on the pavement, has far less chance of receiving a low-tariff sentence than one convicted of wounding, burglary or serious criminal damage. A major factor

Table 4.1 Overall distribution of disposals for each of the categories of offence with sufficient convictions of both males and females to allow statistical comparisons

WOMEN | MEN

% 10 20 30 40 50 60 70 80 90 100 % 10 20 30 40 50 60 70 80 90 100

SUMMARY CRIMINAL DAMAGE
THEFT FROM METER
ABSTRACTING ELECTRICITY
PUBLIC ORDER OFFENCE
WOUNDING
SOCIAL SECURITY OFFENCE
SUBTOTAL: PERSONAL VIOLENCE
DISORDERLY BEHAVIOUR
INDICTABLE CRIM'L AGE
EDUCATION ACT OFFENCE
BAIL OFFENCE
ASSAULT ON POLICE OFFICER
SUBTOTAL: THEFT
THEFT FROM A DWELLING
FRAUD AND FORGERY
TOTAL: IND'BLE OFFENCES
HANDLING STOLEN GOODS
THEFT FROM PERSONS
CRUELTY TO ANIMALS
THEFT FROM VEHICLE
DRUNKENNESS OFFENCES
DOG LICENCE OFFENCES
BURGLARY
THEFT FROM SHOP
THEFT BY EMPLOYEE
DRUG OFFENCES
OBSTRUCTION OF HIGHWAY
SOLICITING/KERBCRAWLING
SUMMARY MOTOR OFFENCES
ALCOHOL LICENCE OFFENCE
PUBLIC TRANSPORT OFFENCE
IND'BLE MOTOR OFFENCES
GRAND TOTAL
DOG LICENCE OFFENCE
TOTAL: SUMMARY
PEDAL CYCLE OFFENCE
VEHICLE LICENCE OFFENCE
OTHER REVENUE OFFENCES
TELEGRAPHY OFFENCE
DRINK/DRIVE MOTOR OFFENCE

Key: //// LOW-TARIFF DISPOSALS   ---- PROBATION ORDERS   ££££ FINES   ▦▦▦▦ HIGH-TARIFF DISPOSALS in these apparent anomalies is the almost invariable use of fines for a wide range of fairly trivial summary offences. Another is the curious treatment of offences of violence, which are typically treated more leniently than offences against property. Table 4.1 also illustrates the overall sex differences. Low-tariff sentences are conspicuously commoner in the female distribution, while high-tariff sentences are conspicuously rarer. Part of this discrepancy can safely be attributed to objective differences in the patterns of male and female offending. A larger proportion of female offenders are 'first offenders', and as such are less liable to some of the severer penalties. It may also be the case (although this is more problematic) that even within each category, the worst types of offences tend to be committed by males rather than females. Some additional factors which contribute to this discrepancy will be discussed in the following section.

In the case of fines, the trends are more ambiguous and the sexual discrepancies more varied. Commonest, particularly among the indictable offences, are the categories in which females receive a significantly smaller proportion of fines than do males. These include criminal damage, disorderly behaviour, fraud, forgery, and most of the categories of violence against the person. In all of these, the male and the female rates are separated by at least ten percentage points. The most straightforward way of describing such trends is in terms of a direct reluctance to impose fines on female offenders, which would naturally tend to squeeze female offenders into the various alternative sentences. But corresponding to this, there also appear to be more positive considerations involved, actively favouring these alternatives. First there is a greater willingness to use low-tariff sentences for female offenders, which means that the imposition of fines commences rather further along the continuum of female offenders than it does with males. Taking public order offences as an example, no fines are imposed on female offenders unless they fall into the worst 50 per cent of cases. In male cases, by contrast, the imposition of fines begins in the first quarter of the spectrum. Second, there is a greater readiness to put female offenders on probation, which means that the imposition of fines tends to be somewhat curtailed at the further end of the spectrum. For female drug offenders, for example, the proportion of probation orders is more than double that of males, although the proportion of higher-tariff sentences is similar: one has to conclude that these orders are primarily displacing fines. At either end of the scale, there is thus a greater use of individualized sentences. At the lower end, women are squeezed out of fines and into conditional or absolute discharges. At the other they are squeezed out of fines and into probation.

The categories in which women receive a *larger* proportion of fines than men do are few, and can be dealt with more straightforwardly. The only category in which the difference amounts to more than a few points is that of indictable motoring offences, in which 73 per cent of female cases result in fines as compared to only 53 per cent of male ones. In this category neither low-tariff disposals nor probation contribute significantly to the distribution for either sex. Virtually the whole of this discrepancy is accounted for by the deficit of high-tariff sentences for women: put crudely, female offenders receive more fines because they escape most of the sentences of imprisonment that are imposed on men.

Between these two poles are the cases where the total proportion of fines is loosely the same for male and female cases. Here one sees the balance of all the factors identified above. In the low to middle end of the spectrum, there is the direct reluctance to fine women, coupled with the relative preference for low-tariff sentences, which ensures that the female fines commence rather later than the male. But at the high end of the spectrum, this is compensated by the relative reluctance to imprison women, which not only swells the proportion of probation orders for women, but also squeezes some of them back into fines.

In all these disparate cases, one unifying point can therefore be emphasized. Regardless of the similarities or dissimilarities in the ultimate *proportion* of offenders receiving fines for particular categories or groups of offence, it is never the same *range* of offenders who make up the figures. The female fines are invariably displaced towards the more serious end of the scale. Women generally go on receiving low-tariff sentences well past the point in the spectrum where men start to receive fines. And in certain cases, they then go on receiving fines at the stage when men start receiving imprisonment. It is this disparity which underlies – and undercuts – the apparently neat coincidence in the overall proportions. There is parity in the figures but not equity in the distribution.

Paradigms of gender: the moral economy of fines

In the preceding discussion I have taken the liberty of attributing a logic of motives to the statistical patterns. I have spoken, for example, of a 'reluctance' to fine or imprison women, a 'preference' for individualized sentences for them, and a 'readiness' to put them on probation. In so doing, I have jumped the gun of my own argument: to derive such motives from the figures alone is at best speculative and at worst circular. In this section, however, I shall endeavour to make amends, by illustrating more directly the reasoning that underpins the statistics. Here I focus on two types of material. First, drawing from individual criminal cases, there are the arguments and evidence offered by the various professionals who contribute to the decision on sentence.[3] This material includes recommendations from social inquiry and medical reports, information from the prosecution, speeches in mitigation, and statements from the Bench. Second there is material from interviews with members of these professions, relating more generally to the factors that influence their conclusions. Both bodies of material illustrate the professional concerns which inform the 'logic' of sentencing, and which provide, within the terms of that logic, the adequate and acceptable reasons for decisions recommended or made.

From the outset of this analysis, there are important imbalances in the data. The crimes for which fines are most commonly imposed are the *summary* offences, a broad classification which includes not only a number of relatively serious crimes, such as public health offences, but also many very trivial ones, such as obstructing the pavement with a dustbin. Unfortunately (though significantly) these are precisely the cases where one finds least material relating to the choice of sentence, in either male or female cases. Summary offences are almost invariably tried in magistrates' courts, and generally at considerable speed. Sometimes the defendant will have pleaded guilty by post and will not even appear in court. Few defendants will have any legal representation beyond that of the court's duty solicitor, who will have learnt of the case only on the day of the trial, and whose 'speech in mitgation' will necessarily tend to be scanty. Social inquiry reports are rarely prepared for these cases, and medical reports are almost unheard of. Often the only factors which can enter the decision on sentence, explicitly or otherwise, are the brief facts of the offence, and the sex, address, and criminal antecedents of the offender. It is unsurprising, therefore, that in pronouncing sentence in such cases, magistrates rarely offer more than the most perfunctory indication of any deliberations underlying their decisions.

The trivial nature of many of these offences, the routine pattern of their processing, the scantiness of any formal deliberation, and in most cases the absence of much significant sexual bias, would all make it easy to overlook their importance to the current analysis. To ignore them would be a mistake, however. If nothing else, the sheer volume of these cases lends them an overall importance. More than 80 per cent of all criminal trials relate to summary offences, and of these, more than 85 per cent result in fines. In total, such cases account for 90 per cent of all the fines recorded under criminal law. In arguing for any major reduction in the overall number of fines, it is therefore imperative to look for reductions in this area. Furthermore, an attention to the reasons for the overwhelming use of fines for summary offences provides some significant insights into sexual discrepancies in the field as a whole. For evidence in this area, I rely almost wholly on interviews with practising magistrates, since there is little documentary evidence for such cases, and other personnel very rarely contribute to the decision-making.

Put simply, the magistrates took for granted that fines were simply the 'normal response' to most of the wide range of summary offences coming before them. None of them volunteered any major advantage of such sentences, although one mentioned that the imposition of a fine (by contrast to a low-tariff sentence) would ensure that the offender 'knew he had been punished' and another referred in passing to the possibility of deterrence – while going on to assert that the 'normal fine' was probably too small to deter. Several made comments to the effect that the constant use of fines was 'not very creative' or 'not very satisfying', but equally well, they seemed largely indifferent to any *dis*advantages of fines: they repeatedly insisted that the amounts involved were small (though this is presumably a matter of perspective) and that in the unlikely event of a fine's causing hardship, the offender could usually pay by instalments. In contrast, the other options were presented as fraught with special problems, and only appropriate in special cases. Low-tariff sentences might invite a lack of respect for the court, and an undesirable sense of having got off scot-free. Probation was time-consuming to arrange, expensive to administer, and unlikely to be justified for a trivial offence, especially as many probation officers refused to recommend probation in cases not liable to imprisonment. High-tariff sentences were not available for many of these offences, but were in any case also seen as expensive, as rarely justified in relation to summary crimes, and as particularly likely to result in the personal embarrassment of the decision being taken to an appellate court and overturned. Fines by contrast were the 'opinion of default': in the absence of special reasons for any other sort of disposal, the only question was how large the fine should be.

These observations point to an important rule of thumb: the more quickly a sentence is passed, and the fewer 'special considerations' are allowed to enter the decision, the more likely it is that a fine will be imposed. As described, the impact of this principle is particularly evident with summary cases, where there is rarely more than the most cursory deliberation, and where fines are the almost invariable outcome. But it is also evident with more serious offences, which generally receive rather more detailed consideration at sentence. For these cases the rule can be stated more provocatively: the more care and attention is given to the sentencing, the less likely it is that a fine will appear useful. In a general way, this rule is reflected in the very much lower rate of financial penalties for indictable crimes. It is also reflected quite directly in the documentary material and courtroom speeches. Amongst the cases examined, there was a consistent correlation between the volume of material available and the likelihood of a non-financial penalty. Financial penalties were scarcely ever imposed in cases where there had been long reports or speeches; in cases where they were imposed, there had often been no reports at all.

This rule of thumb has an important impact in relation to gender. Right across the board, but particularly with more serious offences, sentencers tend to give more detailed attention to female cases than to male. There are a number of reasons for this. Women account for less than one in seven of all offenders tried, and they thus tend to stand out as relatively unusual, and to excite more than average curiosity. By the same token, sentencers are often conscious of their own lesser experience in dealing with them, and are accordingly more ready to seek additional advice before reaching their decision. To compound this, popular prejudice suggests that female offenders are more likely than male to have 'abnormal' reasons for offending, whether social, psychological or medical, and are therefore more likely to require special assessment. The same notions are bureaucratically embodied in various Home Office recommendations,4 which have consistently urged sentencers to pay particular attention to the treatment of female offenders, and to arrange for the preparation of social inquiry or other reports in all but the most trivial or uncomplicated of cases. In turn, the same factors influence those who prepare the reports: those on female cases are generally therefore both longer and more detailed than comparable reports on males (Allen, 1987: 35–51). As a result, at the point of sentencing a woman, magistrates and judges often have access to a far more complex body of information than would be available in a comparable male case. In the remainder of this section, I shall be describing some of the concerns that structure this material, and which lead, directly or indirectly, to the characteristic pattern of less punitive and more individualized sentences for the women concerned. What must be emphasized first, however, is that the actual content of such material is only half of the story. It is often its very presence, almost independently of its content, that seems to disrupt the normal routine of fining, and forces open the door to the consideration of other approaches. The more retributive treatment of most male cases, which forms the backdrop of comparison to this analysis, could rarely be attributed to any comparable body of material in which mitigating factors were raised but rejected, or were supplanted by others. What was striking about the male cases was that so little of such material was ever present at all.

I alluded earlier to four interrelated tendencies likely to influence the distribution of fines for female offenders:

1 direct reluctance to fine women
2 a readiness to use low-tariff sentences
3 a relative preference for probation
4 a relative disfavour for high-tariff sentences.

There is often considerable overlap in the arguments raised in each case, since in each there is a call for either a lenient or an individualized approach, and the distinction is often blurred. However, these four considerations will provide a useful schema by which to organize the discussion that follows.

Can't pay, shouldn't pay: the reluctance to fine
When sentencers think about such matters at all, they seem inclined to reason rather differently about the economic capacities of male and female offenders. Some of the resulting disparities in treatment are realistic and relatively unexceptional. Most obviously, the fines imposed on female offenders tend to be smaller than those imposed on males, which is consistent with the typical differences in their economic circumstances and earning power. Taking crimes of violence against persons, for example, female offenders are more than twice as likely as males to be sentenced to a small fine (less than £25), and less than half as likely to be sentenced to a large one (£100 or over).[5] Equally 'realistic', though somewhat more disturbing, are

the different approaches towards the parental responsibilities of male and female offenders. The majority of adult female offenders have children, and a large proportion of these mothers are unsupported and rely on state benefits. That such women simply *cannot* pay a financial penalty is frequently made quite evident both in social enquiry reports and in speeches in mitigation. Even employed mothers are often earning so little that a financial penalty is acknowledged to be unrealistic:

> *Defence Counsel*: 'Mrs A has a daughter who is just under three; there was a previous child, a son, who was a cot death. . . . Mrs A is separated from her husband and there are continuing disputes both with him and with the DHSS about maintenance for the child . . . the simple fact is that nobody pays. The flat is damp and uninsulated and the child suffers from asthma, which means that a very considerable part of my client's income has to go on heating. The gas and electricity bills are in arrears; prepayment meters have now been fitted for both, and in addition she is paying off the arrears at £5 per week each. She cannot work without the childminding, and that is another £15. There are also hire purchase debts for the furniture, which is in her name, and for additional clothing and other items for the child. Including Child Benefit, her net income as far as I can ascertain is between £60 and £70 per week, and the regular bills come to £48, the remainder needing to be spent on food and other items. I think under the circumstances, it would be most difficult . . .'
>
> *Magistrate*: 'I see where you are driving. It does not appear that a financial penalty would be viable. She's in breach of the conditional discharge but there's that child to think about. Stand up please Madam.'
>
> (Evidence in court: woman convicted of theft)

It is obviously realistic to recognize that the ultimate responsibility for children is commonly borne by mothers rather than fathers, that unsupported mothers often have no resources to pay a financial penalty, and that in such cases the imposition of any fine can only result in further debt, poverty, or offending, and that the children will suffer. Sadly this 'can't pay, shouldn't pay' reasoning is largely restricted to single mothers, and 'good mothers' at that. In the case of mothers cohabiting with men, and also of prostitutes, there is often the cynical assumption that if need be they will 'get the money from somewhere', and the court is often none too careful in enquiring about where. In sentencing fathers, however, there is typically even less regard for the impact of a fine. Whereas the status and responsibilities of motherhood are regularly emphasized, those of fatherhood tend to be treated as peripheral. Thus, for example, statements relating to parental responsibilities were three times more frequent in social inquiry reports on women with children than on men with children.

Amongst the fathers, it was only in quite exceptional cases (such as that of a man who was supporting ten children and an invalid wife) that family responsibilities were accorded major emphasis either in court or in the reports, or had any noticeable impact on the demands of punishment. More commonly, the attempt to argue against a financial penalty (or indeed a prison sentence) on grounds of its damaging impact on the man's children or family tended to be met by the traditional argument from the Bench that 'he should have thought of that before committing the offence' (Thomas, 1979: 211–13).

Additionally it is assumed that even where a man has very limited income and considerable family responsibilities, he will normally retain sufficient funds for his own entertainment, and that this portion of his finances can therefore be confiscated without loss of his family. The following, for example, is addressed to an unemployed man with a common law wife and three children, all living on state benefits.

> *Magistrate*: 'I don't want to see you before this court again, do you understand? You were out drinking on the afternoon in question and I think we should put a stop to that. It's time you got a job. Miss B, here [Probation Officer], tells me that you have difficulty making ends meet. Well you shouldn't be out drinking. You don't seem to be short of beer money. There will be a fine of £30 on the first count and £25 on the second. £55 in all . . . You'll have to talk to Miss B about payments before you leave today. Until you get a job you'll have to stay home and forget about your drinking parties, and that will be no bad thing.'
> (Speech in court: to male convicted of theft and disorderly behaviour)

Beyond these comments, it appears that no consideration is given to the likely impact of the fine upon the offender's four dependents, whose welfare is already jeopardized by his habitual drinking and the poverty of state benefits. The implication that the fine will be paid from his 'beer money', thus converting him into a domesticated husband and father, is a piece of such shabby sophistry as to be hardly worth criticizing.

Displacing blame: the move down-tariff

The second factor modifying the use of fines for female offenders is the greater willingness to deal with female cases by means of low-tariff disposals. In some cases these disposals entail the potential for future punishment in the event of reoffending, but in the mean time, they require no immediate intervention or privation. In principle, one might expect the summary offences to provide the widest scope for such treatment, since many of these relate to quite minor misconducts. In practice, however, low-tariff disposals are rarely imposed without some exercise of special pleading, and as outlined already, the circumstances of summary trials tend to preclude this. Paradoxically it is therefore in relation to the more serious offences, where decision-making tends to be slightly more complex and leisurely, that the possibility of these disposals is more commonly raised.

Sometimes the special pleading is directly related to the pragmatic issues discussed above. Where the poverty of the offender makes a financial penalty impracticable, a conditional discharge will sometimes be imposed simply as a matter of expedience. More often, however, the special pleading is concerned with the *ethics* of punishment. Both technically and in the eyes of criminal justice personnel, the low-tariff disposals are in some sense 'less than sentences'. In arguing for a disposal that is somehow 'not quite a sentence', the commonest tactic is therefore to present the offence as similarly 'not quite a crime', or the offender as 'not quite a criminal'. The following is a typical example:

> *Defence Counsel*: 'As you can see from the probation report, Miss C has recently succeeded in establishing herself in a stable life-style, despite great personal difficulties, as a respectable member of her new community, a good neighbour, and a good mother. For some months she has supported herself and her daughter by running a small shopping agency, which is used by many of the local old folk and can actually be regarded as providing a service to the community. . . . Her little daughter is currently having to be looked after by a friend, and is waiting for her outside the court today. . . . What happened on the 15th of September is something she cannot properly explain, though if I may say so, many people would find her reaction understandable, in view of the great tension she was under at the time, with her daughter unwell, the child's father away and unable to offer support, and what appears to have been a degree of provocation from Mrs D [the victim]. . . . She is deeply remorseful about what happened, and as you will have read in the medical report, she is full of self-blame. One might feel, in fact, that she has been punishing herself rather more than the events themselves would merit. For it must be recalled that this incident began as no more than an honest disagreement, in which my client had only reasonable interests at heart.'
>
> (Speech in mitigation: woman convicted of assault)

The speech effects four displacements. First, there is the displacement of the woman's identity as a criminal: she is instead a good neighbour, a good mother, and good citizen. Second, there is the displacement of the offence as a violent crime: instead it is merely an 'event' that has 'happened', an unfortunate but 'understandable' twist to an 'honest disagreement'. Third, there is the displacement of the woman's responsibility for her behaviour: she herself cannot properly explain what she has done, but speaking for her, the defence counsel attributes it to blameless circumstances outside her control – her tension, her daughter's illness, the absence of her partner, and provocation by the victim. Finally there is the displacement of the penal system as the locus of punishment: if there is any need for punishment, then she has already been more than punished through her remorse and self-blame. These four displacements, echoed in two social reports and a statement from her doctor, serve to neutralize the demand for punishment: the woman is awarded an absolute discharge, and is bound over to keep the peace.

In principle, such manoeuvres are equally open to male offenders, but in practice, they are conspicuously commoner among female ones. As I have described in more detail elsewhere (Allen, 1987: 88–108), the characteristic construction of female cases enhances the potency of such tactics. In female cases, there is typically less emphasis on the woman's external actions and more on her internal experiences. Indeed, the sense of the female offender as the active perpetrator of any crime tends to be obscured by a portrayal of her as essentially a passive creature, who is somehow 'carried along' by events over which she has little influence. At the same time, the focus on the inner life of the female offender, the self-fulfilling search for psychopathology, and the appeal to 'emotional traumas' as both the cause and the effect of offending, all facilitate the displacements I have described. Precisely the converse points may be made about male offenders. The emphasis tends to be on their external and material lives, and their emotions are rarely explored or even considered. They are typically assumed to be active, intentional creatures, whose actions speak for themselves. Such characters are the 'normal criminals' of judicial discourse: in a case peopled by such subjects, it is relatively harder to gain credence for displacements like the above. Instead it is much easier to treat their 'normal crimes' as meriting 'normal sanctions', and so the tariff effectively begins at the level of the fine. The statistics in this instance are eloquent enough. Amongst those convicted of indictable offences, one in four women are awarded these low-tariff disposals. Only one in ten men are similarly treated.

Asserting concern: the move for probation
For the offender who might otherwise face a considerable fine, the mechanisms just discussed have obvious advantages. There are potential pitfalls however. With only minor changes of emphasis, the same arguments that serve to push many women down tariff will also serve to push others up tariff, into probation. As mentioned earlier, probation orders are made almost twice as often in female cases as in males, and in female cases tend to appear rather earlier in the total spectrum: just as low-tariff sentences tend to replace fines at the lower end of the scale, probation orders tend to replace them at the higher end.

The arguments are straightforward, and follow closely on those already described. Each of the factors which invite a lesser degree of condemnation may also each give reason for *concern*. If the offences arise from the offender's inward or outward problems, then will she not continue offending until these problems are resolved? If she is at heart a worthy citizen, does she not deserve guidance in extricating herself from these troubles? If she is greatly suffering, should she not be given help? If she has drifted into crime through the lack of wholesome influences or the presence of corrupting ones, then would she not benefit from someone to 'advise, assist and befriend' her? In short, can it be enough simply to exempt her from active punishment, by making a low-tariff disposal? In view of all the reasons for this exemption, should not the court be doing something more?

Again, these are lines of reasoning which are in principle equally open in relation to male offenders, but which in practice have more immediate currency in relation to female ones. They depend on a whole series of notions about the vulnerability and dependence of the subject, all of which fit more easily with stereotypical conceptions of the female offender than the male. Male offenders tend to be credited with a kind of crisp, uncomplicated, self-explanatory criminality. In reports and speeches on male offenders, criminal histories and behaviours tend to be reported matter-of-factly, as if requiring no special explanation: presumably they steal because they are dishonest and acquisitive; they fight because they are aggressive; they ignore authority because they don't much care about it. Such a conception of criminal personhood tends to be uncongenial to the special pleading for probation just as it is uncongenial to the special pleading for lenience.

In female cases, by contrast, the notion of criminality tends either to be compromised by a portrayal of the woman as essentially passive and unintentional (as described above), or else to be problematized by the search for underlying psychological meanings. It is this which provides the ground on which arguments for probation can take root. There is a readiness to see female offenders as psychologically vulnerable, needy, emotional and only equivocally or incidentally criminal. In place of any crude calculus of acquisitiveness and aggression, it is normal in the professional discussion of female cases to recognize contradictory motivations, different levels of intentionality, multiple social pressures, and the ambiguous nature of the offender's relationship to authority. A woman's acquisitive offence can equally be interpreted instrumentally, as an attempt to resolve objective problems, or expressively, as an attempt to call attention to them. Her conflicts with authority may as easily be read as evidence of her desire for boundaries, as indicating her hostility or indifference to them. Her violence towards others will frequently be presented as more to do with love or self-defence than with hostility or aggression. Against the complexity of such assessments, a decision simply to discharge the offender can seem as unhelpful and irrelevant as a fine. The assertion that the offender is causing problems only because she *has* problems tends to undermine a straightforwardly punitive approach, but it can equally undermine the non-interventive approach of the low-tariff disposals. As in the illustration below, which relates to a first-offender convicted of shoplifting and assault, a recommendation of probation can seem the obvious move.

Defence Counsel: 'You will see, Sir, that whereas the psychiatrist says the medical history can't fully explain what happened on this day, it plainly goes a great way towards explaining what is a unique and very unfortunate incident in the life of this woman. She has many interests and . . . does a lot of voluntary work and is well-known to the local social workers as a result of this work. . . .

She is hitherto without blemish on her character. She is deeply upset and ashamed. About the punch thrown – it seems she didn't understand what was happening and thought she was being man-handled and reacted rashly. The punishment she has undergone as a result of the proceedings are obvious here today. It is quite traumatic. Whereas a suspended sentence and fines are appropriate remedies in the face of serious charges, I would suggest they are not likely to do much good, and indeed may do a great deal of harm. What I would like, would recommend as appropriate, is a probation order. The social worker is able to comfort [*sic*] her to face the situation, and I understand the social workers in E are more than willing that she should become subject to a probation order and possibly a direction to maintain regular contact with her psychiatrist and GP . . .'
Magistrate: 'We feel a probation order is appropriate.'
(Discussion in court: woman convicted of theft and assault)

Of itself, the reasoning is kindly, but in the practical context of current penal trends, its implications are unfortunate. Traditionally probation orders were established to provide an alternative to *any* sentence, as a 'free floating' disposal, unrelated to the standard tariff. Over the past decade, however, both courts and the probation service have increasingly called for the use of probation orders to be restricted to more serious cases, where a term of imprisonment would be the alternative sentence. This objective is also emphasized in the recent Green Paper (Home Office, 1988a). The effect is thus to constitute probation as a relatively high-tariff disposal, after which the logical next step, if the offender should again come before the courts, is a custodial sentence. The 'arguments of concern' that can at times, as described above, serve to push seemingly vulnerable offenders out of fines and up into probation, may thus ultimately hasten their journey towards imprisonment.

Rewriting control: from imprisonment back to fines
The final difference in the use of fines for male and female offenders is related to the relative reluctance of the courts to impose prison sentences on women. The only category of offence in which this trend seems to be unambiguously registered in the statistics is that of the indictable motoring offences (where the very much smaller proportion of high-tariff sentences for women is precisely offset by the very much higher proportion sentenced to fines). There are a number of other categories, however, where fines are still used

for female offenders at a point in the overall distribution at which males have moved on to high-tariff sentences. As illustrated in Table 4.1, these include wounding, assault on the police, bail offences, and a variety of summary categories. In many of these cases, even the *consideration* of a high-tariff sentence may have been precluded by the kinds of factors already discussed. Occasionally, however, the movement 'down-tariff' is more overt and explicit, as in the following extract. The offender concerned has set fire to her over-insured and unwanted car, and then collected the insurance. The scope for mitigation is slight. The offence was carefully premeditated. The woman is 24, childless, employed, and has no history of privation or hardship. She has spent the money on personal items and a holiday. She has previously been on probation but was 'breached' when she consistently failed to keep contact. As the probation report observes, it is a case which must inevitably attract a punitive sentence:

> It is difficult to make a recommendation in this case. It must be admitted that Miss F has a considerable history of delinquency, stemming back to her late teens when she left home. The court will undoubtedly be considering a custodial sentence. With this in mind, I have referred her to the CSO, and she has been found willing and suitable for such an order, but there are currently no appropriate opportunities available, and in any case, she is fully employed so would only have restricted availability for Community Service. I would point out, however, since the offence Miss F has returned to live with her parents, and they have been in frequent contact with my department since they found out about this charge, and they may certainly be regarded as exercising a degree of control and supervision over her at this stage, and her employers are also aware of the situation. Miss F has gradually become aware of the gravity of the offence and the period in custody prior to bail being granted has certainly heightened her sense of the seriousness of her situation. Under all the circumstances, I would point out that Miss F is in a position to pay a considerable financial penalty from her employment, as well as repaying the sum dishonestly obtained, and in view of her youth, employment, and home situation, I would respectfully recommend that this possibility be considered in this case.
>
> (Social inquiry report: woman convicted of fraud)

Amongst the cases examined for this discussion, there were seven female cases and three male cases which fell into this category: in each of these it was openly acknowledged that a custodial sentence was the 'obvious choice', but in each case a financial penalty was recommended and eventually accepted. The three male cases were all quite different from each other, and included highly individualistic 'special pleading'. The seven female cases, however, had several important points in common. They all included elements which undercut the kinds of defences and mitigations discussed above: these were never impoverished mothers of dependent children; they had not committed crimes which could easily be presented as impulsive or only half-intended; in each case they were the main instigators and beneficiaries of the crime; and although all had criminal records, none appeared socially deviant in other respects. This last point seemed particularly important. Whereas in the majority of female cases it was the *assertion* of multiple problems which was used to legitimize special treatment, in these cases it was the *denial* of multiple problems. All of these women came from relatively comfortable, undisturbed backgrounds, and apart from the offending, they all led relatively conforming lives, with respectable jobs, homes and families. Against this background, their offending was presented as definitely deviant, indisputably culpable, but probably containable and controllable. The choice of a financial rather than custodial sentence reflects these two concerns: a relatively weighty fine is presented as providing a punishment component comparable to that of a high-tariff sentence, whilst the family or other informal agents would be called upon to supply the component of control and containment. In the background of all of these cases there were close and respectable relatives who were presented in reports or mitigation as being ready to exercise some kind of authoritative influence. In most cases these were parents or husbands; in one they were a son and daughter-in-law.

The interpretation is obvious and sociologically familiar (Kruttschnitt, 1982; Eaton, 1983). In the final analysis it is not even unrelated to the considerations discussed in previous sections. Men are constructed as the primary subjects and agents of a public world, socially constituted in terms of their material relationships and behaviours, and governed by the formal rule of law. Women, by contrast, are subjects of a double set of controls. It is not that they are without material obligations to a public world, or able to escape entirely from the formal control of the law. But first, they are judged as subjects of a more private world, socially constituted in terms of their emotional relationships and responsibilities, and governed by the informal rule of the family. The recognition of this double (and potentially conflicting) status modifies the relationship between women and the criminal justice system. At times, as discussed in the earlier sections, it enables this system to make allowances for pressures which tend to be discounted in male cases, or to intervene in areas of personal trouble which in male cases would not even be examined. At other times, as discussed here, this recognition enables the criminal justice system to impose less conspicuous formal constraints, in the confidence that the rule of the family will impose these constraints instead. As has long been observed (e.g. Chesney-Lind, 1978) it is only those women who have conspicuously lost or rejected or transgressed these informal controls, who experience the criminal law in its full force of coerciveness and constraint. The treatment of such doubly deviant women deserves serious consideration in its own right (Carlen, 1983b; Carlen et al., 1985), but it is not with this minority of cases that this chapter has been concerned.

Passing judgments

In seeking to expose some of the sexual 'paradoxes and paradigms' that affect the use of financial penalties, my aim has been critical as well as analytic. Under English law, men and women are formally constituted as equal, and as equally subject to the same laws and the same range of penalties. In practice, of course there are differences (Allen, 1988). There are differences in what the law formally demands of them, differences in how the law assesses and judges them, and differences in the pattern of penalties that they receive. Whether these differences are desirable or oppressive is a matter that has to be judged in individual cases, and perhaps judged differently for different occasions and different purposes. There is certainly no easy calculus. From a Utopian perspective, the objective of formal equality, that men and women should be judged on precisely the same terms, has an appealing ethical robustness. Yet to treat this as an uncompromising imperative can produce more inequities than it resolves. Legal practice simply cannot afford to ignore, for example, that outside the formal domain of the law, women and men do *not* take equal responsibility for children; that men and women are *not* subject to equal constraints or equal opportunities; that perhaps they are not even equally responsive or vulnerable to particular forms of treatment or punishment. There is the risk, if one demands no more than formal equality, of achieving treatment that is formally identical, but whose practical consequences are far more punitive for one sex than the other. There is also the risk of merely extending to both sexes the disadvantages that were previously restricted to one. The proposals that follow attempt to steer a survivable course between these two risks. They acknowledge that there are sometimes good reasons for the 'special treatment' that is accorded to women, and attempt to preserve the advantages that such treatment offers. At the same time, they attempt to extend this treatment to men where it seems that this also might have advantages, and to counteract those aspects of it that depend on unhelpful and unnecessary conceptions of gender. All of the proposals derive directly from the substantive material in the main body of this chapter.

My first proposal is only indirectly related to questions of gender, although it springs directly from the discussion above. I suggested that the massive disparity betweeen indictable and summary offences in the use of low-tariff sentences is the product of two factors: that fines are currently the 'sentence of default' for these crimes, and that the circumstances of summary trials make it rare for the court to hear of any special factors that might justify a departure from this treatment. This results in the absurd situation in which very minor offenders are less likely than very major ones to receive low-tariff sentences. *I propose that the very basis of this situation should be examined, reviewed and changed*. On the basis of the case material, I posited the 'rule of thumb' that there is an inverse correlation between the number of personal factors taken into consideration by the court and the likelihood of a fine being imposed. It seems entirely likely that if the courts *were* to investigate the circumstances of summary offenders more carefully, they would find just as many 'special considerations' to be taken into account, and that in a vast number of cases the kinds of factors that are emphasized in female indictable cases, would also apply to summary offenders of both sexes. It is entirely unlikely, however, that either the expense or the personal intrusion of such investigations could be justified in these cases. Instead, as a measure of compromise, *I propose that in view of the minor nature of many summary offences, the 'sentence of default' in such cases should become a low-tariff sentence rather than a fine, and that it should therefore be the higher tariff sentences, including fines, which would then require the justification of special considerations and unusual circumstances.*

Second, *I propose that much greater attention should be given to the sentencing of male offenders in general, in particular to those convicted of serious offences.* I suggested, on the basis of the same 'rule of thumb', that part of the sexual discrepancy in the use of fines is related to the relatively greater attention that is given to the sentencing of female offenders. A comparable attention to the personal lives and circumstances of male offenders might allow the courts to identify a far larger proportion of male offenders who could appropriately be dealt with by less punitive means. The current official guidelines emphasize the importance of social inquiry and other reports in female cases, but these tend to be the cases which are already guaranteed a degree of special attention, simply on the basis of popular prejudice. *I suggest that this gender bias in the guidelines is therefore at best redundant, and that official policy should instead emphasize the importance of obtaining comparable information on offenders of both sexes.*

Third, *I propose that there is need for a special status of probation order, to be made in those cases where the primary intention of supervision is to offer formal support and guidance to an apparently vulnerable offender who might otherwise be eligible for a low-tariff sentence.* Many practising probation officers recommend such orders, many sentencers see them as the ideal option for vulnerable offenders, and they are a regular feature of female sentencing. However, the current Green Paper reinforces the current trend of treating probation as effectively a high-tariff sentence, almost on a level with imprisonment. Against this pressure, two outcomes seem plausible. One is that such orders will indeed be effectively squeezed out. I believe (although aware that this is a contentious point – Millard, 1982) that the loss of such orders would often be to the personal disadvantage of the offenders concerned, and to the general detriment of the criminal justice system. The other alternative is that probation orders *will* continue to be made in these cases, but under a formal rubric that makes little or no allowance for them. The risks already noted would then be amplified: the attempt to offer help and protection to the vulnerable will all the more easily accelerate their journey up-tariff. The provision of a specific and distinct low-tariff probation order might circumvent these risks. In the immediate term, for reasons discussed above, such orders have a particular currency for female offenders, and it is they who would most immediately benefit. In the longer term, there is no reason why such orders should not be more widely considered for male offenders also.

Fourth, I would emphasize that punitive sentences, including fines, appear consistently earlier in the total spectrum of male sentences. In some cases this may be justified by 'objective factors' such as the longer criminal record of many male offenders or the serious nature of some of their offences. But the evidence from female cases indicates that it can be viable to sentence even quite serious offenders, and even those with considerable criminal records, in less damningly punitive ways. *I propose that the positive evidence of the whole distribution of female disposals should be taken into account in every review of sentencing policy.* This distribution should lend weight to existing arguments which suggest that in many cases imprisonment could be safely avoided altogether, and punitive sentences replaced by more lenient and rehabilitative ones.

Fifth, and underpinning each of the above, *I propose that more emphasis should be given to the responsibility of sentencers to consider their own sexism, and to question the different expectations that they bring to the judgment of male and female offenders.* In speaking of this as a 'responsibility', I am not referring to the general and essentially political point, that in some sense they owe this to 'society'. In other contexts I would cheerfully endorse such a claim, but my argument here is more restricted. As I have described, legal agents frequently make a whole variety of gender-determined assumptions, which influence the choice of sentence. That these legal agents have a 'responsibility' to question and challenge such assumptions can properly be asserted not only on broad political grounds, but also on more narrowly legal ones: it is a responsibility imposed upon them by the formal requirements of their own discourse. For the best part of a century, English law has enshrined a principle of the legal equality of the sexes: male and female subjects are for legal purposes to be considered equivalent, bound by the same laws and judged in interchangeable terms (Interpretation Act, 1978). If legal agents are to be bound by this doctrine, they are under obligation to exclude from their reasoning the ordinary prejudices that would subvert its operation.

Without denying the limited and problematic nature of this legal responsibility, I suggest that its assertion may allow a significant tactical leverage. The recognition that principles of sexual neutrality and equality do already have a place in legal discourse makes it immediately legitimate to urge sentencers to give attention to these matters, and establishes at least a minimal rubric for complaints based on sexual disparities. It opens the door for some of the objectives I have outlined to be pursued through existing legal channels, including, most obviously the appellate courts. *I propose that these courts should be urged to take every opportunity to establish clear and explicit precedent against sexual disparity in sentencing.* For example, it should be formally established that prior to sentence, the courts have the same obligations to inform themselves about the personal circumstances of offenders of either sex, and that those mitigating factors which are commonly considered in relation to one sex should be given equal weight and consideration in relation to the other. Correspondingly it should also be more clearly established that anyone who has been sentenced to a severer sentence than would ordinarily be awarded to an offender of the opposite sex has adequate grounds to appeal. Sentencers at all levels should be called upon to incorporate into the mental gymnastics of their reasoning the question of whether, if the offender had been a member of the opposite sex, they might have sought other or additional information, interpreted certain matters differently, given more weight to one consideration or another, and ultimately have reached a different sentence. I suggest that against the current pattern of sentencing, the effect of such attention would be registered initially and primarily in decisions which increased the use of low-tariff and individualized sentencing for male offenders. It would bring the issues raised by such sentencing more clearly into the public and judicial eye, and ultimately it would allow a political evaluation of the changes of sentencing practice that I have here proposed.

Notes

1 That is there are more female convictions than male for this offence, and males receive a larger proportion of low-tariff sentences, a smaller proportion of fines, and a higher proportion of probation orders. The differences are tiny; only their uniqueness lends distinction.

2 All categories for which there were fewer than 100 convictions for each sex have been omitted. A few categories of similar offences with similar distributions of sentenced have been combined. With the exception of figures mentioned in Note 5, all statistics in this chapter are derived from *Criminal Statistics: England and Wales 1987* (Home Office, 1988b) and relate to offenders aged 21 and over.

3 Most of these cases were collected in the course of my own PhD research, which was funded by a grant from the Economic and Social Research Council (Allen, 1987). Additionally, Dr Joanna Shapland kindly allowed me to use a number of court transcripts collected for her research on mitigation (Shapland, 1981).

4 For example Home Office Circular 29/171, which is still endorsed in the current advice to courts.

5 These figures are drawn from 1986 statistics, as the relevant volume of the 1987 statistics had not been published at the point of writing. They also refer to offenders of all ages rather than aged 21 + , as the published statistics on this topic include no separate breakdown by age.

5
Fraudulent justice? Sentencing the business criminal

Michael Levi

Introduction

I shall be concerned in this chapter principally with questions of fairness in the punishment of white-collar criminality. It has long been accepted that the original formulation by Sutherland (1983, originally 1939) of 'white-collar crime' as a crime committed by persons of high socio-economic status in the course of their occupational activities contained at least one key conceptual flaw in conflating the social status of offenders with the social interests that were affected by their malpractices. This conflation equally tends to be present in radical work which contrasts the treatment of low-status offenders with that of high-status offenders (sometimes unconvicted), irrespective of whether the prestigious offenders victimize the poor or the rich, large corporations or smaller ones.

Recent attempts to operationalize and test notions of class bias in criminal justice have sought to eliminate this conceptual ambiguity, but at the risk of eliminating important intra-class differences. (There are some major problems in their class-ification process which I shall not elaborate in detail here.) For example, Hagan (1988: 3) complains that the Sutherland definition of white-collar crime 'not only shifts attention away from corporations as the units of study, it grounds the measurement of class position in gradational notions of "respect" and "status".' By contrast, he seeks to reinstate the centrality of structural measures of class position, grounded in relations of ownership and authority, for 'owners of businesses and persons with occupational authority are located in positions of power that allow use of organisational (usually corporate) resources to commit larger crimes than persons located in employee positions without authority' (Hagan 1988: 4). However, although such an approach is conceptually clearer, would measures of class really make that much difference compared with measures of status? It is undoubtedly the case that

> employers are becoming quite adept in using the power that derives from their structural location in the social organization of work to distance and disengage themselves from the crimes that they nonetheless encourage subordinates to commit. . . . The effect is to leave the latter more open to the application of criminal sentences.
>
> (Hagan, 1988: 9)

Yet ironically, and unmentioned by Hagan, it is with regard to questions such as how people in apparently *lowly* positions obtain relative immunity from prosecution that a concentration on power relations rather than formal status yields the most obvious explanatory benefits. As the work of Mars (1982) and Ditton (1977) – not to mention Sergeant Bilko films! – on workplace fiddles indicates, modest-ranking manual and clerical workers may exert considerable control over production and service delivery, and may be allowed to get away with continuing frauds that are substantial in relation to 'normal' predatory crime by *outsiders* against people and organizations, even if they are not very substantial compared with frauds committed by corporate executives.

A number of important questions might be asked about sentencing in 'white-collar crime' cases. Is there a general level of sentencing, and what is it? What influences sentencing decisions? Is there discrimination in favour of (or against) 'white-collar crime' (compared with which other types of crime or social class groups of offenders)? What is the *effect* of punishment upon fraudsters? There is a comparative paucity of information with which to answer these questions, and some of them – such as the issue of bias – can be understood only in the context of the 'criminal selection procedures' in the policing and prosecution processes discussed elsewhere (Levi, 1987; Cook, 1989 and Chapter 6 of this volume). For these determine the prestige – or degree of 'upmarketedness' – of those who come before the courts for sentencing. The more sophisticated and active the policing and prosecution process against sophisticated fraud in any area at any given time, the more likely it will be that there will be a representative base for judging the fairness of sentencing across the board. There is much room for dispute about how far western countries have moved in the direction of prosecuting elite white-collar criminals – a category whose boundaries are very hard to determine – but it is my contention that there have been important changes in this respect, even if there remain very substantial inequities in the susceptibility of different sorts of offences to the prosecution process. These inequities include the *de facto* immunity of corporate executives from manslaughter charges for health and safety 'homicide' (Wells, 1988).

North American research on sentencing

In the 1970s, before the more open-ended views of Gramscians about the forms and consequences of class control largely replaced the clear predictions of conflict and traditional Marxist theory, sentences on business-people were crudely compared with those on the normal proletarian or *lumpenproletarian* output of the criminal courts: see, for example, the social critiques of Reiman (1979) and Snider (1982). However, North American sentencing research began to develop far more subtle analyses of the factors that influenced white-collar sentencing, or rather that subset of it that related to *financial* crime. (Matters like health and safety sentencing were bifurcated off into the category of 'corporate crime' and subsequently ignored, even though the motivation for pollution and poor health and safety may be equally profit-maximizing as that for insider trading or bribery.) An interesting shift occurred in the process of developing these explanations of sentencing. North American studies of 'fairness' in punishment of securities violators (Benson and Walker, 1988; Hagan, 1988; S. Wheeler *et al.* 1982; 1988) use samples of white-collar offenders convicted under criminal statutes (including securities laws) as the unit of analysis, rather than the broader category of acts *legally* described as socially injurious and for which a penalty was provided, as favoured by Sutherland (1983). If the Sutherland approach were adopted, we might incorporate those 'securities violators' who are dealt with by other disposal methods, including closure of their firms by regulatory authorities, civil disgorgement of profits (e.g. for Financial Services Act 1986, rule-breaking other than insider trading, which is not covered), suspension of some firm members, and administrative tribunal fines, censures and reprimands. These are important aspects of dealing with violations *outside the criminal process* as quasi-fines and restitution. This is quite additional to civil lawsuits. In short, the methodology adopted by the sentencing sophisticates has the advantage of looking only at those people who have been adjudicated guilty in the criminal courts – thus disarming critics who object that white-collar crime may amount simply to corporate conduct to which radical criminologists take exception – but this advantage is also its *dis*advantage in eliminating from the data set precisely those high-status corporate managers who are believed by radicals to benefit most from the 'prosecution selection' process. (Though whether they benefit or are singled out for exemplary punishment because of their newsworthiness is itself a contentious issue.)

Hagan (1988: 26) observes that the decision to charge under either the Canadian Criminal Code or the (non-criminal but imprisonable) Ontario Securities Act is important, since although there are no statutory minima and 57 per cent of those convicted under the Criminal Code receive less than the one-year maximum under the Securities Act, those convicted under the latter tend to receive lighter sentences. The data suggest that managers are treated with disproportionate severity and employers with disproportionate leniency. In his analysis of differential sentencing, Hagan focuses upon

1 the increased tendency of employers *not* to want to know *how* their subordinates achieve profit targets so long as they *do* achieve them, thereby not incurring liability for themselves but not discouraging it in managers
2 the relative ease of proving a specific securities charge than of a more emotive criminal charge in a complex case, complexity being greater the higher the class of the 'offender'
3 the positive relationship between 'offender' social class and international-ization, which makes employer cases more expensive to investigate fully and thus less likely to be prosecuted as crimes
4 in his conclusion, the possibility (1988: 39) that there may be some violation of the relative autonomy of law in ensuring that employers were *not* charged with criminal code but rather with securities code violations (i.e. there was some sort of political 'fix').

Some US studies (reviewed in Levi, 1987: chs. 7 and 8) find that although up-market white-collar criminals are less likely than other federal offenders to be incarcerated, once they *are* imprisoned, they generally receive a tough sentence. This can be affected by the socio-political climate within which sentencers operate: for example, Hagan and Palloni (1986) *did* find a 'Watergate effect' on imprisonability, though Benson and Walker (1988) found that this was true only of some parts of the USA. As I shall argue, this upwards pressure on white-collar sentences occurred in the UK also in the 'fraud scandal era' of the late 1980s.

The sentencing of fraud in England and Wales

A superficial examination of sentencing trends reveals that over the period 1979–87, the number of males over 21 given sentences of immediate and partly suspended prison sentences for fraud and forgery at Crown Courts rose from 1,300 to 2,100. There was a very slight drop (with fluctuations both up and down in the interim) in the *proportion* of males convicted *at Crown Courts* who were imprisoned – 48 per cent in 1979 and 47 per cent in 1987 – and it appears that the rise in numbers imprisoned is attributable not to increased judicial punitiveness *per se* but rather to the increased numbers being convicted and to the introduction of partly suspended prison sentences in 1982. Separate figures for females were not kept until 1982, but the number of females over 21 imprisoned at Crown Courts for fraud and forgery rose from 175 in 1982 to 239 in 1987: in both years 28 per cent of those convicted (and note the low absolute numbers imprisoned). (Without controlling for offence seriousness and previous convictions – which may make a marked difference – there is a much lower imprisonment rate for fraudulent women than for men.) The peak year for fraud imprisonment was 1985 for men and women.

In 1987 the principal sentences imposed at all courts for commercial fraud offences were as shown in Table 5.1 (Home Office, 1988b). This relative absence of imprisonment for fraud in courts overall would apply *a fortiori* to those convicted of 'regulatory fraud' offences. For example, in the year up to September 1987, 30 people were imprisoned in the United Kingdom out of 4,692 recorded convictions in relation to offences of fair trading and consumer protection violations (Office of Fair Trading, 1988).

Table 5.1 Sentencing of fraud in 1987

	Frauds by company director	False accounting	Other fraud	Bankruptcy offences
Fine	21	236	6,582	65
Suspended prison	21	116	2,171	24
Partly suspended imprisonment	13	17	294	6
Unsuspended imprisonment	21	68	1,696	12
Youth custody	1	2	213	0
Total	83	626	18,733	152

As for the *length* of sentences, in 1987 only nineteen people in England and Wales received sentences in excess of four years for fraud (compared with fifteen in 1986). As we move down the length of sentence scale, we find 43 (40 in 1986) imprisoned for more than three and up to four years, and 149 (119 in 1986) imprisoned for over two and up to three years for fraud. Four people were jailed for more than two years for false accounting (compared with four in 1986 and none in 1985). In fact, for males over 21, the average length of sentence for fraud and forgery has dropped over the period 1979–87: from 17.1 months to 14.5 months at the Crown Court, and from 3.7 to 2.9 months at magistrates' courts. (The effective length of imprisonment is lower still since, as I will show later, fraudsters are matched only by handlers of stolen goods in their success in the parole stakes.) So although the number imprisoned has increased, their average time inside has decreased, thereby keeping the fraudster prison population in equilibrium. Even if we set aside the fact that fraudsters are disproportionately likely to go to open prisons – which are under capacity – it is clear that given both their numbers and the length of time they are serving, commercial fraudsters are not creating the crisis of overcrowding in the English penal system!

Are fraudsters' hit hard in their pockets instead of being deprived of their liberty? The fines imposed are far from draconian. In England and Wales in 1987, the average fine for fraud and forgery was £89 for men and £69 for women in magistrates' courts and £316 for men and £128 for women in Crown Courts. In that year, only twenty-eight men were fined more than £1,000 – less than the median post-tax monthly salary for lawyers and business-people – and a further twenty-eight men and the woman were fined over £750 up to £1,000 for fraud and forgery. Taking all sentences for insider dealing and for making fraudulent multiple share applications in the 1980s up to January 1989, only two fines have exceeded £10,000.

It might be argued that fines are low because the state does not want to deprive the offender of the means to repay the victim and/or because the victim will pursue the offender through the civil courts. Compensation and reparation are increasingly highlighted as key features of penal policy – see Part VII of the Criminal Justice Act 1988 – though their value as alternatives to imprisonment for fraud may be limited by appellate rulings that the period of repayment should not normally be greater than twelve months: *Ramsey* (1987) 9 Cr.App.R. (S.) 251. In 1987, even before sentencers were required by the Criminal Justice Act 1988 to consider compensation, those convicted of fraud and forgery were more likely than any other property offenders to be made to pay compensation: 47 per cent in magistrates' courts and 17 per cent in Crown Courts. The average compensation ordered was £144 in magistrates' courts and £5,030 in Crown Courts. In 1987, out of 7,941 ordered to pay compensation at magistrates' courts, 118 were ordered to pay £751–£1,000, and 151 more than £1,000. Of 1,012 fraudsters and forgers required to pay compensation at Crown Courts, 61 had to pay £751–£1,000 and 222 more than £1,000. Perhaps these do adequately reflect the more financially serious white-collar crimes, but there is no way of telling. They may – and legally should – reflect offenders' (perceived) means as much as victims' financial and emotional losses. The criminal statistics cannot tell us anything about civil reparation, but informed sources state that except where the convict is a business-person with substantial assets and/or is pursued by a revenue department, civil redress against *convicted* persons is comparatively rare: it is more common as an *alternative* to prosecution, where it is believed that the suspect has the means to repay the debt.

Although the annual criminal statistics and reports of government bodies are far from helpful in illuminating either the social standing of those sentenced or even the vaguest outline of the nature of the frauds for which people were sentenced, it is possible to disaggregate from other sources what happens to *some* sub-types of fraudster. In 1987–8 163 people were fined an *average* of £25,438 for Value Added Tax evasion (though no data are now available for the proportion imprisoned, which in 1986–7 was 15 per cent of those convicted). A further 229 VAT fraud cases were settled (with the agreement of the 'offenders' and at a criminal burden of proof) without prosecution by compounding, but details of these administratively imposed quasi-fines are not revealed. The Inland Revenue does not provide any details regarding sentences. The Department of Trade and Industry (DTI) does not reveal prison sentences imposed on the twenty-eight people convicted for fraud-related companies offences.

The case of 'regulatory' offences should perhaps be considered separately, since although the non-supply of financial information may be a cover for fraud and skimping on health and safety may be motivated by greed and/or economic precariousness, they are not fraud and may be defined by sentencers as 'inadvertent', partly because mitigated guilty pleas and the lack of need to prove intent mask the seriousness of the offences. This is equally true of fair trading offences: see the interesting account by Croall (1988) of the way in which legally represented corporations effectively downplay their culpability compared with unrepresented sole traders.

Whatever the reason, the financial penalties across the range of 'regulatory offences' tend to be low. In 1987–8 the average fine for failure to furnish annual returns to the DTI was £70 and for failure to deliver accounts was £78: less than the cost of two hours of an average accountant's time! (These offences cover a wide range of seriousness, but the *maximum* fine is £2,000.) As regards acts encompassed by the Office of Fair Trading (including those enforced by local trading standards officers), the following are the fines imposed on those convicted during the year up to September 1987. (The figures are deduced from information supplied by the Office of Fair Trading, 1988.) Fines for false descriptions of goods averaged £580 (plus £42 compensation). Other average fines and compensation were for false price claimed, £636 (plus 20 pence compensation); false statements about services, £467 (plus £50 compensation); Restrictions on Statements Orders, £253 (plus £28 compensation); Business Advertisements (Disclosure) Orders, £348; Consumer Credit Act, £382; Estate Agents Act, £2,000 (but only one conviction); Weights and Measures Acts, £388 (plus 8 pence compensation); Food and Drugs Acts, £351 (plus 23 pence compensation); Hallmarking Act, £148; Consumer Protection and Consumer Safety Acts, £438 (plus 37 pence compensation); Shops Act, £848; Road Traffic Act 1972 (relating to unroadworthy vehicles), £257 (plus £61 compensation); and other trading and environmental health legislation, £325 (plus 7 pence compensation). In 1987 the average fine overall for offences reported to the Office of Fair Trading was £441: in recent years, this average has increased by more than the rate of inflation. The average fine imposed for all violations prosecuted by agencies under the Health and Safety Executive was a record £794 in the period 1987/8 (compared with £410 in 1986/7 and £189 in 1981). However, this rise occurred solely because BP were fined £750,000: without this, the average fine would have been £420 in 1987/9.

There is some relationship between scale of offence and penal sanctions in tax fraud cases, which applies to the risk of being imprisoned but not to the size of fines. The Keith Committee (1983) found that the arrears: fine ratio was 23:1 in larger cases and 2:1 in smaller cases, possibly because big fraudsters are jailed. That committee reviews sentencing practices somewhat drily:

It appears that the congested state of the jails does not allow so many convicted tax fraudsters as formerly to be awarded an immediate custodial sentence. It has been suggested that fraudsters should be fined substantial sums in lieu of custodial sentences, but there is no indication from these statistics that the courts have adopted this approach. Indeed, compared with the scale of culpable arrears, the fines imposed in the larger cases are modest. . . . The recovery of arrears in prosecution cases . . . is slow and difficult . . . given the circumstances and scale of the larger tax frauds, it is questionable whether such sentences have significant deterrent value.

(Keith Committee, 1983: 357)

However, formal penal sanctions are not the only sorts of sanctions that are applied to commercial malpractice. Also significant are the wide range of 'regulatory' punishments – some court-imposed, others not (though increasingly subject to judicial review) – that arise in a variety of commercial and professional contexts. These will be reviewed briefly below. (See further Levi, 1987: chs 7 and 8.)

Disqualification orders

An important and interesting type of punishment is the order which disqualifies a person from taking part in the management of a company or from a particular profession or occupation. In Britain and the USA prohibition from entry into business because one is not a 'fit and proper person' may occur in many areas: gaming, insurance, financial services, the law and accountancy professions, and the police. None of these is restricted to using convictions as a *necessary* condition of the prohibition, nor is conviction (particularly when the offence involves driving or alcohol) always a *sufficient* condition for being banned: the Rules of the Securities and Investments Board, for example, require disclosure only of those criminal convictions 'connected with investment business or of a financial nature'. From the occupational group's standpoint, the prohibition on employment is properly viewed as an incapacitation sentence: the limited evidence on whether or not it actually does incapacitate is examined elsewhere (Levi, 1987: ch. 8). However, there are circumstances under which the *courts* can impose disqualification.

As a matter of form, disqualifications are not viewed as being fundamentally penal. Yet as Browne-Wilkinson VC observed in *Re Lo-Line Electric Motors Ltd*. (1988) 2 All ER 692, they do involve a substantial interference with freedom. It seems to be agreed that the primary purpose of disqualification is protection against dangerousness, not retributive. Yet 'in a normal case, the conduct complained of must display a lack of commercial probity, although in an extreme case of gross negligence or total incompetence, disqualification could be appropriate' (ibid.). There remain unresolved conflicts as to what level of incompetence or what breaches of commercial morality are required to justify 'unfitness': see *Re Stanford Services Ltd* (1987) BCLC 607. *A priori*, it is unclear why negligence or incompetence are less predictive of future losses to creditors than lack of probity: morals may be easier to change than incompetence! This conceptual unease suggests the mixture of motives – retribution, general deterrence, special deterrence, or incapacitation – that may actually underlie disqualification orders.

The courts – as contrasted with commercial/professional bodies – are empowered to impose commercial disqualifications under two sorts of circumstances: as a sentence at the time of conviction; and in response to requests from liquidators or the Official Receiver, which may or may not follow a conviction. The legal aspects of disqualification are discussed in detail elsewhere (Levi, 1987: 218–21 and 345–6; Dine, 1988). Magistrates' courts can impose bans up to a maximum of five years; Crown Courts up to fifteen years. Without a specific research study, it is impossible to ascertain the number of fraud cases in which disqualification orders *could* have been made, but if we aggregate all the legislation under which disqualification can be made, we note a rise and then levelling off of them: in 1983, there were 89 orders; in 1984, 128; in 1985, 120; in 1986, 124; and in 1987, 197 orders (of which 171 were made under the Company Directors Disqualification Act 1986). So although increasing use has been made of the power to disqualify, it is utilized still only modestly in relation to the volume of directors whose companies go bust. (My earlier study of sentencing in all long-firm fraud cases at the Old Bailey revealed that in the period 1951–61, disqualification orders were made against 22.1 per cent of offenders; from 1962–1972, this actually dropped to 18.1 per cent – Levi, 1981).

Moral fault does appear to be an important ingredient not only in taking action but also in determining the length of disqualification. Save for menial or low-status clerical jobs, what a disqualified person *can* lawfully do in the (proportionately increasing) *private* sector remains obscure. As to the length of disqualification, judicial perceptions of sincere efforts at rehabilitation appear to be critical. A director of six British companies who was fined £650 after defaulting on the obligation to supply accounting material on 100 occasions was disqualified for four years under what is now Section 297 of the Companies Act 1985; he made no attempt to remedy the situation: see 2 *Co.Law* 174. By contrast, in *Re Civica Investments Ltd.*, (1982) 126 *Sol Jo* 446, (1983) BCLC 456, a disqualification order of only one year was imposed in the light of the substantial efforts of the director to remedy the 'failures' which led to his prosecution. In respect of 'planned' frauds, in *R* v. *Austen* (1985) 1 BCC 99, 258, the Court of Appeal took a very hard line, confirming a ten-year disqualification upon a motor trader who had defrauded finance companies of some £300,000 by making false hire purchase applications and similar devices. Following conviction for VAT fraud involving £5 million, the two principals were disqualified for ten years, and five- and three-year disqualification orders were imposed upon two others convicted of a lesser role (*Financial Times*, 17 November 1987): *prima facie*, this too looks like a mixture of incapacitation and retribution. The point here is that although the monitoring of what happens to disqualified persons is very slight – they are unlikely to find their way on to Regional Crime Squads 'target of the month' list! – the financial implications of disqualification can be very serious and are perceived to be so by senior executives (Levi, 1987).

Sanctions imposed by self-regulatory organizations

It is too early to provide information about fines imposed by self-regulatory organizations under the Financial Services Act 1986. However, this can be a significant dimension of non-court punishment. In Britain in the period 1984–8, Lloyd's has completed twenty-four disciplinary cases covering fifty-two individuals. Of these ten have been expelled (in a total of six cases); one has been totally excluded and another has been given a lifetime exclusion from transacting business; twenty-six have been suspended (including four for life). Additionally – some offenders receiving multiple punishments – there have been fourteen censures, twelve reprimands, and eight fines (averaging £226,562). The expulsion of one member – Ian Posgate – was reduced by the Appeals Committee headed by a Law Lord – Lord Wilberforce – to a suspension for six months (though Lloyd's subsequently refused to accept his re-registration as an underwriter on the grounds that he was not a 'fit and proper person': so he might as well have been expelled). It should be noted that Lloyd's requires proof at the criminal standard of certainty, though a criminal jury may have a different conception of what certainty entails. Here again, there may be little sympathy from readers, but *to the extent that activities actually are curtailed*, the loss of up to £1 million pounds annual income can hardly be dismissed as an insignificant punishment, though how significant it is may depend on the wealth and expenditure levels of those sanctioned. Furthermore, as in the case of disqualification of directors, many executives are in the game for power and prestige as well as money, so banning them from trading is a punishment in itself (though its effects are hard to estimate with any accuracy).

Accounting for sentencing levels

The task of explaining levels of sentencing is beyond the scope of this article. Popular responses (as well as some criminological literature) attribute it to class bias or, less culpably, to cultural homogeneity between judges and business-people (Sutherland, 1983). However, as I have argued elsewhere (Levi, 1987; ch. 7), even if we exclude as irrelevant that judges do not *perceive* themselves as 'protecting their own', the bias hypothesis fails to take into account the fact that most victims are relatively wealthy and few convicted fraudsters come from any elite that judges might have a supposed interest in protecting.

Amongst those factors that may be important in explaining sentencing levels are that particularly where the accused pleads guilty, both crime seriousness and offender culpability tend to be minimized by the fact that in Britain, sentencing is not really an adversarial process. (There is a contrast here with the USA and many European countries, where prosecutors present sentence recommendations, often accompanied by sentencing memoranda.) White-collar sentencers commonly are faced with *offences* that they may consider grave, but *offenders* who are often described as having 'excellent characters' (even if this means that they have no convictions rather than that they are moral exemplars in social conscience). The highest status defendants have in the past tended to be moderate-ranking solicitors who have 'invested' at the expense of their clients' accounts. In such cases (and most others involving professional people with no prior record) the lines of mitigation are clear-cut: disqualification and loss of community standing indicate severe moral and economic suffering; the money was spent to sustain a declining practice or gambling, or else resulted from marital stress rather than from greed; the defendant has paid back as much as he can or has sold his home, and (where foresight is absent!) this is not a case where he has salted away the proceeds in a foreign bank account. These are usually offered as reasons for sentencing below the tariff for whatever kind of offence has been committed.

Sometimes, however, ingenious lines of mitigation are found, as in such allegedly 'morally ambiguous' crimes as making multiple applications for shares using false identities. For example, in September 1986 three directors of companies in the Portland Group were fined £750 each on each of six summonses of attempting to obtain British Telecom (BT) shares by deception. They had attempted to make a total profit of some £1 million and had actually made at least £95,000 by submitting at least 1,500 applications for shares in BT, which were expected (correctly) to be massively oversubscribed, attracting a large premium on the offer price when dealings commenced on the Stock Exchange. Such a major sum could be expected to attract a substantial prison sentence had the case been treated as 'real' fraud. Yet defence counsel said in mitigation that the BT prospectus had not given any warning that the making of multiple applications – which he described as 'a hallowed practice in the City of London' – might be treated as a criminal offence and observed that

> It is a very strange philosophy that says, after the event, it is a crime to put in multiple applications but on the other hand, if the issue is under-subscribed, we will add them all together and adopt them.

This was part of former Conservative MP (and barrister) Keith Best's defence in his plea of not guilty, as well as in his mitigation when convicted. It presumably found favour with the Court of Appeal, which quashed his prison sentence and substituted for it an increased fine. (In November 1988 a solicitor was imprisoned for this offence, the only one to date.) However, one problem counsel have in presenting mitigation is that they cannot always predict whether a line of argument will count as mitigation or as aggravation. For example, the longest English fraud sentence I have found is one of fourteen years – reduced on appeal to eight years – upon *Higgs*, a 40-year-old management accountant (earning a mere £8,400 a year) who defrauded his US parent company of over £3 million over a five-year period, turning the subsidiary from a profit-making to a loss-making concern. The accountant also ran a book-making business, but spent virtually all the money gambling unsuccessfully himself: during 1984, he staked £889,000. The sum involved clearly was very large, though not by the standards of some operations in the City of London, but no one (except the plant manager, an innocent whose signed cheques were altered by the accountant) lost his job. The only tangible benefits of his fraud were a detached house in a wealthy part of Cheltenham, a new car for his wife, and public school (i.e., in Britain, private) education for his three children (costing some £300 a term). He sold his house to repay the company. The size of the fraud plainly owed much to the lax financial control system of the US company as well as from his actions, and in some cases (of fraud against banks) this has counted as mitigation, as has the fact that the money was spent gambling rather than for profit (thus allowing an argument of 'diminished moral responsibility'). As Higgs put it, after he had been caught, to the parent company's accountants: 'It was not a devious conspiracy thing. I fell into a spiral trap. I used a flood of Prestolite funds to repair the damage.' Some judges might have imposed a short prison sentence, or even a disqualification order plus a probation order combined with a requirement to attend Gamblers Anonymous. Yet here, the sentencing judge appeared to regard none of these features as mitigating his culpability, stating

> We are not dealing with the Great Train Robbery but a simple theft from your employers, but the amounts involved are simply miles beyond any legal authority. You did this with your eyes open to feed your gambling habit.
>
> (*The Times*, 22 March 1986)

Another feature that historically – until the suspended sentence imposed upon insider dealer Geoffrey Collier in 1987 – may have been significant in accounting for sentencing in fraud cases is the lack of hostile media publicity about 'the low level of fraud sentences' in Britain (though not in the USA). It is hard to predict any particular sentence from any particular set of facts about a case: were the non-gambling solicitor and self-employed builder who received two years and two and a half years' imprisonment respectively (*The*

Times, 18 June 1986) for masterminding a plot to swindle banks of £1 million only one-seventh as culpable as Higgs, who initially got fourteen years? Even in an appellate case, a fraudster with no previous convictions could be given four years' imprisonment on the basis of the gravity of his offence, or given a six-month sentence on the grounds that he had already suffered professional disqualification and we should keep offenders out of lengthy custody wherever possible. (In a trial court, he might expect less than that. For further discussion of the role of appellate courts in relation to fraud, see Levi, 1987; 1989.)

Sanctions upon corporations themselves present different considerations from sanctions upon natural persons, for the fear of causing unemployment reduces sentences even where the offence is viewed gravely. This applies not only to pollution and to health and safety offences but also to frauds. In December 1980 Mr Justice Jupp, sentencing a subsidiary of the textiles company Gannex Ltd in relation to an international fraud of over £500,000 upon the Customs and Excise, almost £190,000 of which could not be traced, observed

> Unfortunately, I have come to the conclusion that punishment will fall upon the innocent. There are people working in these companies whose jobs are in jeopardy. . . . It is going to be poor comfort to them if the Court imposes a fine which closes a factory and causes anyone to lose his job.

He imposed a fine of £375,000 (plus £93,000 costs) upon the company, which was reduced on appeal, and whose payment still remained outstanding in 1986, the revenue finally agreeing to accept staged payments. Lord Kagan himself was sentenced to ten months' imprisonment, fined £105,000, and disqualified for three years – including his spell in prison – from taking part in the management of a company: in mitigation was his plea of guilty and the fact that he had spent three and a half months in a French jail, albeit resisting extradition, so this could hardly be represented as repentance. As a 'surprise' bonus, charges against his wife and son were dropped since, as prosecution counsel observed, 'the prosecution of this matter would have been prolonged, difficult, and costly'.

Do commercial fraudsters receive discriminatory treatment?

The term 'discrimination' is not used in a morally neutral way: it implies that differences exist in the treatment of different people that are *unjustifiable*. The notion of disparity assumes that we are comparing like with like, and it is precisely this that is so difficult. What do we mean by 'like'? It is one thing to argue over whether or not any given sentence or sentencing policy is 'too strict' or 'too lenient'. It is quite another to say that one set of sentences for one crime is unfair compared with a set of sentences for another type of crime.

Moreover, the interpretation of differentials in one way rather than another is subjective. If we were to show that commercial fraudsters were sentenced more leniently than burglars of commercial premises, but that first-offender commercial fraudsters were sentenced *less* leniently than first-time commercial burglars, what would this show? We might equally well counter that pound-for-pound stolen, first-time fraudsters got off more lightly. And what if 'fairness of punishment' incorporated a notion of the impact of punishment upon different offenders? How would we weight the loss of *em*ployment prospects for the convicted fraudster against the continued *unem*ployment prospects of the typical convicted burglar? Or the 'pains of imprisonment' for a lawyer versus those for his more typical client? There are plainly a number of difficult empirical and conceptual problems here. Indeed, though not generally presented as a 'class justice' issue, retributivists disagree about whether to include such 'relative deprivation' psychological impacts in their judgments about what different offenders 'deserve' (Singer, 1979; Von Hirsch, 1986).

There is also the question of non-court sanctions to consider. The punishments imposed by the Stock Exchange and by Lloyd's cannot include imprisonment, nor do they carry the stigma of a criminal conviction – though as Posgate found, being refused readmission to Lloyd's as *not* a 'fit and proper person' has major effects – but there was no clear evidence at the Stock Exchange that higher-status 'offenders' were sentenced more leniently. They enjoy a structural favour, inasmuch as partners who are suspended from entering the floor of the exchange nevertheless continue to enjoy their share of the partnership income, so what looks like a severe punishment may not affect their earnings (apart from the extra profits that their presence might have brought). By contrast, their lower-status associates lose their livelihood if they are suspended. But setting aside these critical economic consequences of censure, and quite apart from what sentencers *say* about the greater moral turpitude of malefactions by senior personnel, partners actually were normally given more severe *formal* penalties in multi-defendant cases.

Let us examine the statistics on sentencing in England and Wales in relation to offence convicted. In 1987 the proportion of offenders given an immediate custodial sentence was 35 per cent for burglary, 77 per cent for robbery, 11 per cent for theft and handling stolen goods, and 15 per cent for fraud and forgery. In each year of the 1980s, fraud has attracted the second lowest percentage of over-21s sentenced to imprisonment at the Crown Court for crime for gain, the least-imprisoned category being theft and handling stolen goods.

As regards length of sentence, average figures are not available, but in 1987, well over half the fraudsters sentenced to unsuspended imprisonment in the Crown Court received sentences of twelve months or less. The median sentence was the same – twelve months – for burglary and for theft and handling stolen goods, but was four years for robbery. In magistrates' courts, half the fraudsters received sentences of three months or less, the same as burglars and thieves. However, these figures are slightly misleading because fraudsters are less likely to be imprisoned and are *more* likely to be given partly suspended prison sentences than burglars. A crude but interesting comparison is that the number of people jailed for longer than four years – the cut-off point for the label of long-term imprisonment – in 1987 included 19 people for fraud, 17 for forgery, 31 for theft, 12 for handling stolen property, 22 for burglary other than in a dwelling, 84 for burglary in a dwelling (*excluding* aggravated cases), and 666 for robbery. If we focus upon the less emotional crimes (i.e. exclude burglary in a dwelling and robbery) then given the higher average value of frauds compared with other property crimes, it looks as if fraudsters are comparatively leniently treated by the courts.

However, as in the USA, looked at another way, it appears that once the decision to imprison has been taken, fraudsters are not treated particularly leniently. Percentage data from Crown Court sentencing are hard to interpret because they are affected by the choice of jury trial by defendants as well as the seriousness levels prosecuted, but in 1987, at Crown Courts, the rate of *long-term* imprisonment *for those imprisoned* was (in rank order) 36.4 per cent for robbery, 5.65 per cent for forgery, 1.95 per cent for burglary in a dwelling, 1.15 per cent for fraud, 0.73 per cent for burglary other than in a dwelling, 0.64 per cent for handling stolen goods, and 0.61 per cent for theft.

What these data imply in terms of *class discrimination* is rather more mysterious. Among adult offenders, we may take it for granted that nearly all burglars and thieves are working-class and relatively poor. But it would be a mistake to assume that all fraudsters are middle-class: most cheque and credit card fraudsters, for example, are not, and though no separate statistics are kept for numbers convicted, inspection of court records suggests that such 'plastic' criminals are the great majority of those taken to court for fraud.

When we review the question of class *interests*, the position is even more complex. Macro-data from the categories used in criminal statistics are unilluminating: the category 'other fraud' in *Criminal Statistics: England and Wales*, for example, includes everything from credit card fraud to £100 million investment frauds. In the more sophisticated sentencing research on white-collar crime, attempts have been made to examine the relationship between sentence and managerial status/control position in relation to fraud (Hagan, 1988). Hagan found that in respect of Ontario Securities Code offences, higher-status securities violators got off more lightly than others. In my view, part of this may reflect the prosecutorial/judicial perception that included among the lower-status violators may have been those fronting for 'organized crime' figures or even being gangsters. However, irrespective of this possibility, a more class *interest* based analysis of sentencing would look not only at the class of the fraudsters but also at the business interests they affected. Looked at in this way, it is possible to view heavy punishment of high-status violators as rational and expected, since they have both 'let the side down' and risked harming the general level of trading. The difficulty here is how could one ever demonstrate that a sentence was *not* an example of class interest in action? We degenerate easily into tautology.

To the extent that sentences reflect 'the gravity of the offence', and that the monetary cost is part of this, we should note that in 1987, the average value of property stolen in a *recorded* burglary – values in *un*recorded ones being much lower – was £675; in robbery, £1, 379; and in theft (including car theft and unauthorized taking of motor vehicles, 66 per cent of which by value is recovered), £512 (Home Office 1988b). The sums involved in fraud tend to be much greater, which would inflate the average value considerably, though since the majority of frauds appear to be cheque frauds, the median value may be quite low. However, given that Court of Appeal judgments are unlikely to be followed in any consistent fasion by the lower courts, there is no immediate way of comparing high-value theft and commercial burglary sentences with those for fraud. Moreover, 'gravity' is more than just money: it also appears to involve diffuse conceptions such as 'being in a position of trust', the impact upon victims, offence prevalence, and so on. Since all of these factors may run in diverse directions, and no one (including the Court of Appeal) is willing to give guidance as to what weighting should be attached to each, it is hardly surprising that 'offence gravity' raises serious operational problems (see also Fitzmaurice and Pease, 1986: ch. 5; Levi, 1989).

Open and closed prisons: the treatment of fraud

A further element of possible discrimination is the within-prison experience of those incarcerated. White-collar criminals who are unconnected with organized crime groups have a good chance of going to an open prison: better than any other category of offender. For offenders serving sentences of under two years – the majority of those fraudsters jailed – this is a very sharp contrast with the overcrowded local closed prisons, with their poor facilities, and itself constitutes a form of advantage. (A modest *dis*advantage lies in the fact that local prisons are often nearer to home, and therefore make visiting easier.) To be sent to an open prison is also an advantage compared with the tighter security arrangements (and tougher company) in closed training prisons. This is not (or not *just*) deliberate favouritism: it is based partly on predictions of 'dangerousness' should the prisoner escape, and partly on predictions of the *likelihood* of escape. Not only are 'professional persons' less likely to commit offences 'on the run', but also partly for that reason, their escape is less likely to create political heat for prison administrators. Furthermore, to the extent that their sentences are shorter and their confinement conditions more civilized, they are correspondingly less likely to try to escape, particularly if they believe that a closed prison full of 'criminals' and homosexual rapists beckons to them if recaptured: this is particularly true in the USA. Thus, the 'good-risk' image of fraudsters generates conditions of confinement that reproduce the status hierarchy in the outside world and confirm the fraudster's position outside the category of 'the dangerous classes'.

Parole

Although not strictly part of the sentence – a point reinforced by frequent Court of Appeal judgments which refer to the irrelevance of parole prospects to their sentencing appeals – parole is important when reviewing time actually served, and thus the fairness of punishments for different classes of offence and offender. I will not review the *critiques* that have been made about the inconsistencies of the principles applied to parole. Suffice it to note that subject to any changes to be brought about following the report of the Carlisle Committee in 1988, parole applicants in Britain suffer from the 'double sentencing' problem whereby the same criteria used by the trial (and appellate) judges in determining initial sentence are taken into account a second time by the Parole Board and the Home Secretary when deciding whether they are 'fit to be released' before their one-third normal remission date. Retributivist and correctionalist criteria are mixed up in the manner with which we have become familiar in the review of sentencing 'principles'. Thus the *Report of the Parole Board 1986* – and for previous years – states that granting parole

> must be a carefully calculated risk, particular care being taken with the cases of prisoners whose records show that, if they re-offend while on parole their offences may be grave crimes.
>
> (Home Office, 1987c: 15)

Some frauds would be examples of cases 'where the danger is grave':

> A person convicted of more than one sophisticated crime intended to produce a large reward, committed on different occasions, even if violence has not been used or contemplated.

At first sight, this may appear to be confusing offence gravity with risk prediction, but in fact the Parole Board is asserting that it is worse to let offenders out if they appear likely to commit a serious offence than a more minor one. Were it not for the double-sentencing problem, many would find this to be a morally acceptable position. However, since virtually no fraud offenders receive sentences in excess of five years – the cut-off point for grave crimes – they would generally be considered according to the criteria in lesser cases. The *Report* for 1984 stated

> Most prisoners who have committed what is clearly the one offence they will ever commit may properly be granted early parole. . . . There are, however, a few exceptions for whom early parole will be less clearly justifiable. They include . . . notorious cases of fraud or breaches of trust. It can only be said that each case must be considered in the light of the peculiar circumstances.
>
> (Home Office, 1985: 21)

But this was not reiterated in the *Report* for 1986 (Home Office, 1987c).

No particular research attention has been paid to parole in fraud, but we should note that as at the sentencing stage, 'major' fraudsters are advantaged by having typically fewer prior convictions than other substantial property criminals. Given the importance of prior convictions as a predictor of future criminality as well as of retributive deserts, this can be a significant advantage. Equally significantly, the overall background profile of the elite fraudster looks relatively good: the *Report* for 1986 supports this hypothesis when it states (Home Office, 1987c: 12) that other indicators of a high probability of re-offending are 'persistent offending since an early age, short intervals at liberty between convictions and a record of employment which is poor in terms of the quality of the jobs and the lengths of continuous employment.'

Moreover, to the extent that post-release employment prospects improve chances of parole, fraudsters are unlikely to be worse off than other parole applicants: although Breed (1979) points to the difficulties white-collar criminals in prison have in finding jobs (at a time *before* the unemployment rate soared) and, in some cases, to the particular employment problems which result from professional disqualification, they may well be at an advantage compared with other sorts of prisoners. (In the absence of genuine jobs, the really devious can have their friends set up dummy companies to grant them employment: do probation officers or any other report compilers check the employer's records at Companies House?) They are also more likely to have a settled home and relatives waiting for them than many offenders, particularly persistent petty ones. The *Report* for 1987 – like that of 1986 – states

> The home circumstances and employment prospects can be critical for success on parole . . . a good home, a job to go to and the absence of the circumstances and temptations which led him into crime before are factors favourable to parole.
>
> (Home Office, 1988d: 13)

To the extent that criminal records are relevant to parole – and despite the

statements quoted above, the Parole Board clearly thinks they are –
comparing parole rates across categories of offence is slightly misleading, for
one does not know whether any observable differences are due to the
offences themselves or to variations in prior conviction records of people
committing them. Nevertheless, in the absence of any other data, I will
examine offence categories here.

With the (marginal) exception of those convicted of handling stolen goods,
people convicted of fraud have a better chance of being paroled at first review
than any other category of property (or violence) offender: in 1987, no fewer
than 74.9 per cent (76.6 per cent in 1986) of those considered were
recommended for parole, exactly the same as the rate for handling stolen
goods, slightly higher than the rate for theft (72.6 per cent: 71.8 per cent in
1986), and substantially higher than for burglary (64 per cent: 65.6 per cent
in 1986). In 1987 100 per cent of those serving less than a year, 82 per cent
of applicants serving from 1 year to 1 year 11 months, 75.9 per cent of those
serving 2 years to 2 years 11 months, and 71.7 per cent of those serving 3
years to 3 years 11 months received parole on the first review. At the upper
end, only four out of the thirty-six (six out of the thirty-one in 1986)
offenders serving five years or more received parole at the first hearing,
though even that was a much higher proportion than for burglary.

The data from those considered for their *second* parole review include
some who did not make a first application in that year – i.e. relates to a
different prison population – but there were comparatively few fraudsters
left in prison by then: ninety-two (compared with ninety-six in 1986, eighty-
two in 1985 and only forty-eight in 1984). Inequalities between offences had
evened out by the time of the second or further review: in 1987 53.5 per cent
of fraud applicants got parole, compared with 54.4 per cent of burglars,
49.1 per cent of thieves, and 66.7 per cent of handlers of stolen goods.
Perhaps this indicates a bifurcation in fraud between the small 'hard core'
who 'require' incapacitation – 41 parole applicants at second review were
doing five years or more – and the majority who can be released without
danger: 761 at first and 48 at further review in 1987. Altogether, 73.1 per
cent of those fraudsters who applied for parole got it in 1987, very slightly
less than in 1986.

I do not have any data on the length of parole awarded for different
offences – and it can make a considerable difference whether the parole date
is put back for months – but there is no clear evidence of discrimination either
for or against fraud on the basis of the above figures: burglars do worse, but
thieves and handlers do about the same as fraudsters. On the other hand, to
the extent that fraudsters' lack of prior convictions normally will have netted
them a hefty discount in initial sentences, it could be argued that they have
still done much better than other offenders in relation to the gravity of their
crimes. It is impossible to separate out those receiving parole in relation to
prior convictions but certainly, despite the comments of the Parole Board on
the general unsuitability of fraudsters for early parole, there seem to be a

remarkable number of exceptions to this general principle! It is plausible that despite perceptions of the gravity of fraud, they may look like better candidates for parole in correctionalist terms, partly because in most instances, any frauds (other than cheque frauds) committed would be unlikely to come to court – if at all – within the parole period. So again, the more sophisticated forms of fraud enjoy a comparative advantage arising out of their low reporting and prosecution rate. Thus we see British fraudsters generally benefiting from what one might term their low 'evilness rating' – a construct combined from moderate offence seriousness and comparatively light criminal records – and good behaviour inside prison (which in turn is assisted by their often being in open prisons – which have a better disciplinary record – and being not looked upon as 'animals' by prison staff or as challenges to the *machismo* of prison staff or other prisoners).

In the light of the controversy surrounding the release of former champion jockey Lester Piggott just one year and one day after his imprisonment for three years for a £3 million tax fraud, it should be noted that although it may be very unusual to be released exactly as soon as technically eligible, the 1987 figures show that of those fraudsters serving three years but less than four years, no fewer than 71.7 per cent were released on first review, and 61.6 per cent of the remainder released on further review (Home Office 1988d). In short, arguments of deliberate discrimination are hard to substantiate, particularly in a British context. Rather, there is a common mode of rationality from which white-collar defendants benefit, and benefit considerably, compared with those few offenders who steal sums as substantial as do fraudsters.

Conclusions

I am not the first to find the demonstration of sentencing disparity difficult. As Wilkins (1984: 19) in a brief but devastating *critique* of Court of Appeal sentencing 'principles' observes

> The English courts seem to have provided themselves with a defence against any claims to show disparities in their dispositions. There are 'different lines' and/or 'different approaches' which are selected as appropriate, and in addition (or instead?) it is always possible to refer to the concept of 'individualisation'. While we are told that there is 'no single theory', we are not told how many theories there are likely to be – clearly enough to ensure that there is no case to be made by those who would claim to see 'disparity'.

Indeed, the individualization of sentence may justify almost anything, since almost no two offender-crime combinations are precisely the same. I have tried here to tease out part of the sentencing logic of the judiciary – discussed more fully by Ashworth (1983), Ashworth *et al.* (1984), Fitzmaurice and Pease (1986), and, in the context of fraud, by Levi (1987), and S. Wheeler *et al.* (1988) – and to place contemporary sentencing data within the context of that logic. I have portrayed the sentencing of white-collar crime as a more complex mental and social phenomenon that is commonly done in works that attribute differential treatment of rich and poor to elite bias (Reiman 1979; 1984). There are important differences *between* frauds, in terms of impact and who (if anyone) gets harmed, which must be considered along with power and ideology in a proper account of the sentencing process. There are also differences between frauds and those business offences where (truly) harm is not caused deliberately but recklessly. Different *rhetorics* of punishment are used in different contexts: for example, why do sentencers for health and safety violations *not* concern themselves more with general and individual deterrence, as they do when dealing with burglars and robbers? As the Health and Safety Executive (1988: 30) observes:

> it is sometimes disappointing for inspectors, and more seriously it gives the wrong signal to management, when serious failures in health and safety attract relatively trivial fines. . . . we sometimes wonder whether such fines sufficiently reflect the importance which society attaches to the prevention of accidents and ill health.

It seems clear that except for professional people who steal from their clients' accounts – who are almost always sent to jail – fraudsters enjoy a low rate and average length of imprisonment, and a low average size of fine and compensation. Whether this position will change substantially following increased prosecutions of City fraud by the newly established Serious Fraud Office, hardening senior judicial attitudes towards securities fraud, and the Criminal Justice Act 1988 provisions for the confiscation of assets in cases involving more than £10,000 remains doubtful. Quite apart from the impossibility of repatriating assets compulsorily from abroad, it seems to be very difficult for sentencers to treat fines as a *proportion* of offenders' means, rather than as absolute sums, either at the bottom of the scale (in social security fraud) or at the top (in commercial fraud or in 'regulatory' offences such as health and safety or pollution). For instance, following the death of three refinery workers at Grangemouth, British Petroleum (BP) were fined £750,000 in March 1988 by the High Court in Edinburgh for health and safety violations. Yet although this seems like a large sum (and BP would have had additionally to compensate the families of those killed and injured), how great was it in relation to (1) the cost of preventing the circumstances that led to the (undesired) accidents, and (2) the financial assets of BP? This £750,000 fine could mean less to BP than a £100 fine would be someone on social security. In this sense, the Swedish day fine system seems to be necessary as a routine conceptual process for sentencers to undertake if they are to achieve greater fairness (see pp. 41–2). However, both for commercial fraudsters and, to a lesser extent, other offenders, the implementation of that in turn would require us to find out more about offenders' means – including undeclared legal and illegal-source income, and fraudulent preferences to family members in anticipation of apprehension by the police or non-police enforcement agencies – than has hitherto been collected and made available in English criminal courts. (Receivers and liquidators are expert at tracing the disposal of assets and recovering them, but they are paid civil professional rates for this. As I write, the Treasury retains assets confiscated from convicts, thus reducing the incentive for organizational bounty-hunting by the police and Customs and Excise.)

Prior to 1987, there were almost no elite fraudsters convicted in England and Wales, and therefore the possibility of imprisonment did not arise. However, to the extent that elite criminals are less likely to go to prison, this seems less because judges see the offences as non-serious as because offenders have light prior criminal records. As S. Wheeler *et al.* (1988) demonstrate, US Federal judges experience the paradox of high simultaneous offence severity and offender mitigation. They usually try to formulate a total view of the 'white-collar criminal' and sometimes disregard his lack of previous convictions if they believe he has shown no sign of remorse and/or has lied in the witness box. But in general, they see little point in imprisoning to deter convicts from future offending, believing that they are unlikely to reoffend anyway, due to disbarment or prohibition from securities trading and to social labelling. The implication of this seems to me to be that, in white-collar cases, judges weight the prison sentence demanded by retribution and general deterrence against the light sentence implied by the lack of need for individual deterrence. Except for some 'clearly out-of-character' offences, for many working-class or *lumpen* offenders, this equation does not arise so starkly. Whether for reasons of lack of empathy or because sentencers believe that there is less 'natural' tendency among the poor to be law abiding, or both, heavy punishment for *non*-fraud crimes for gain presents fewer dilemmas for sentencers.

Whilst in real terms, the frequently uninsured and burgled inner city poor pay more as *victims* than do businesses, who lose a lower proportion of their assets and can write losses off against tax payable, the poor *offenders* also pay more compared with their wealthier counterparts in relation to their means (as well as in relation to their general alternative life opportunities). Their offences are more likely to be detected; they are more likely to be prosecuted if detected; they build up a criminal record more readily; and therefore in a system where prior criminality is important as an index of immorality, they are more likely to be imprisoned, pound for pound stolen, than is a fraudster. Quite apart from any questions of social and moral equity, this raises interesting implications for patterns of crime. 1987 and 1988 appear to have witnessed an increase in the use of firearms in robberies by 'young tearaways' for whom burglary and less violent theft of cash in transit have become too difficult and/or unprofitable. (Though the clear-up rate of *recorded* crime in 1987 was only 21 per cent for robbery, compared with 27 per cent for burglary and 32 per cent for theft and handling stolen goods.) The richer targets, poorer crime prevention, and lighter sentences in the realm of fraudulent crimes against (as well as by) business have encouraged the more sophisticated members of the 'criminal classes' to move upmarket. The (in my view unintended) consequence is that while Neighbourhood Watch members peer out from behind their lace curtains, and the police or vigilantes patrol outside some of our doors, the fraudsters – elite or humble in their origin alike – are left free to steal the whole street.

6
Fiddling tax and benefits: inculpating the poor, exculpating the rich

Dee Cook

Introduction

The relationships between lawbreaking, wealth, poverty and culpability will be explored here by analysing judicial responses to the 'poor' who defraud the state by fiddling supplementary benefit (now income support)[1] and the relatively 'rich' who defraud the state by evading income tax.[2] The essence of these two forms of economic crime is very similar: making false statements to a government department – Inland Revenue or Department of Social Security (DSS) – to achieve illegal financial gain from the public purse. But the economic and social attributes of the typical offender are very different and this may, initially, seem to confirm the old adage that there is 'one law for the rich and another for the poor'.

Income inequality in itself is not, however, the *sole* factor determining the punishment of tax and benefit fraudsters. 'Taxpayers' and benefit 'claimants' are categories which have been produced by particular histories, and historical discourses have made it possible to attribute entirely different motives to those who fiddle personal tax and those who fiddle social security payments. The comparative analysis which follows will, therefore, start by examining the origins of the contradictory discourses within which it is possible successfully to justify the crimes of those who fiddle taxes, and at the same time denounce the crimes of those who fiddle welfare benefits. It will be argued that such discourses still influence Inland Revenue and DSS policies on the regulation and prosecution of fraud, and are still reproduced in the sentences meted out by the courts. Consequently the ideological construction of 'taxpayer' and 'claimant' both informs and reproduces the unequal and inconsistent sentencing rationales which result in the rich and the poor 'paying' for their economic crimes by very different means.

The 'idle poor'

Historically the poor have been portrayed as idle, feckless and culpable:

> What encouragement have the poor to be industrious and frugal when
> they know for certain that should they increase their store it will be
> devoured by the drones, or what cause have they to fear when they are
> assured, that if by their indolence and extravagance, their drunkenness
> and vices, they shall be reduced to want, they shall be abundantly
> supplied?
>
> (Revd J. Townsend (1786) quoted in Fraser, 1973: 35)

This image, coupled with a powerful invocation of work-incentives, is also
evident in the assumption behind the 1834 Poor Law that 'every penny
bestowed that tends to render the condition of the pauper more eligible than
that of the independent worker, is a bounty on indolence and vice' (ibid.).
The discipline of the workhouse put into practice the Poor Law principles of
less eligibility and effort incentives, as they were designed to deter the
'undeserving' (the able-bodied unemployed) from entering and, hence, from
claiming poor relief.

History certainly repeats itself: these vocabularies and images are still
associated with the 'undeserving poor' in the later twentieth century. For
instance, in 1971 Conservative MP Rhodes Boyson wrote that the cosseting
welfare state made claimants like 'broiler hens' (rather than 'drones'), and he
continued,

> No one cares, no one bothers – why should they when the state spends
> all its energies taking money from the energetic, successful and thrifty
> to give to the idle, the failures and the feckless?
>
> (Boyson, 1971)

In the late 1980s such vocabularies and quasi-explanations for poverty and
economic dependence have become fused in the composite image of the
'benefit culture'. But the essential themes of idleness, fecklessness, culpability
and lack of work-incentives remain unchanged in two centuries. Moreover,
it is a short step, by implication or by design, to encompass 'fraud and abuse'
within the definition of the benefit culture itself and so effectively to link
claiming benefit with *scrounging* (undeservingly or fraudulently) from the
state. For instance, speaking at the 1988 Conservative party conference,
Social Security Secretary John Moore asked:

> It is right that an able-bodied adult can draw unemployment benefit
> simply by signing on once a fortnight without making any real effort to
> find work?

He went on to promise additional measures to ensure yet stricter availability-for-work testing and announced that in 1988 £250 million had (allegedly) been 'saved' through the investigation of 'people cheating the benefit system' (*Guardian*, 13 October 1988). In a similar vein the Employment Secretary Norman Fowler warned, 'I give notice that we are not prepared to see taxpayers' money being used to finance the fraudulent'. But what of the great British taxpayers, in whose name the poor are so rigorously policed? As will be argued below, they are also on the fiddle, but are likely to be defrauding the state of far more revenue than are the 'idle poor', and receiving minimal sanction for so doing (Cook, 1989).

The hard-pressed taxpayer

Disraeli's comment that there were only two inevitabilities in life – death and taxation – illustrates a traditional British hatred of paying personal tax. Thus the image of taxation as a 'harsh inquisitorial system', coercing and interrogating taxpayers and demanding information, dominates the traditional 'old' view of tax (Sabine, 1966). A 'new' view which saw progressively graduated taxation, designed to serve public welfare, emerged in Lloyd George's 'People's Budget' and in post-1945 attitudes to social and economic reconstruction (ibid). But the old view of tax as an 'intolerable inquisition' remains ideologically powerful and sustains the image of the taxpayer as a victim of draconian state regulation:

> Taxation has no merit in itself. It is but a necessary evil and should be limited to the lowest level possible.
>
> (Boyson, 1978: 135)

> People trying to make a go of things get hounded by the taxman . . . the Inland Revenue is bashing the little man.
>
> (*The Times*, 22 June 1985)

These views on taxation inform the vocabularies of motive of those who fiddle their taxes and, when allied to criticisms of the progressive role of taxation, such views may justify illegal evasion in terms of a 'backdoor' tax revolt against the (mis)use of tax*payers*' money for subsidising 'tax-*consumers*' (Burton, 1985: 75). Tax avoidance and evasion can thus be constituted as 'heartening' evidence that the rich can save their wealth from their 'rapacious fellow citizens' (Shenfield, 1968: 26). Clearly such attitudes represent non-compliance to the letter and spirit of the tax laws as strategies for the accumulation of personal wealth. In essence this 'sporting' view of taxation depends on the assumption that 'There are *no* ethics in taxation. There is no moral law in taxation' (Houghton, 1977: 60). Yet issues of morality, culpability and criminality are uppermost when the poor use similar strategies to increase their incomes.

The hard-pressed taxpayer is ideologically constructed as a double victim: a victim of the state bureaucracy of taxation, and victim of the idle poor who are subsidized at the taxpayer's expense. Popular discourses about taxation therefore invariably impinge on issues concerning welfare provision, and so the imagery of the 'benefit culture' does surface in public rhetoric about tax. But it is the image and rhetoric of the 'enterprise culture' which currently dominates tax talk. The 'go-getting' society envisaged and promoted by the New Right demands low taxes, effort-incentives, high rewards, and the 'spur of poverty' for those who fail (Loney, 1986). Rates of tax adjudged to be 'high' are thus anathema to the enterprise culture, and the evasion of such taxes may be represented as in accordance with the spirit of 'enterprise'. Commenting on the growth of the illegal (and tax-free) hidden economy, Mrs Thatcher stated that it was 'big, flourishing, thriving' and meant that 'The enterprise is still there'. (ITV *Weekend World*, 17 November 1985). But when enterprise involves benefit claimants working 'on the side', both the individual's motivations and the economic and social consequences of the hidden economy are perceived very differently.

Givers to and takers from the state

Beneath the images of the idle poor and the hard-pressed taxpayer lie fundamental contradictions between the ideals of collectivism (realized through citizens willingly paying taxes to finance state welfare) and individualism (realized through the entrepreneurial spirit and the accumulation of personal wealth). If the latter perspective is adopted then tax revenues evaded are seen to belong to the *citizen*, who merely fails to pass them on to the over-regulating state. This view of the taxpayer as 'giver' to the state profoundly influences policy relating to the prosecution and punishment of tax fraudsters. If, by contrast, the former perspective is adopted, taxpayers who fiddle are seen as failing in their part of the citizenship bargain with the state, yet they still retain the economic status of 'givers'. But whichever perspective is adopted, the benefit *claimant* must always be constituted as a 'taker' from the state and, ultimately, from the taxpayer. The punishment of benefit fraudsters is rooted in their negative economic and social status as 'takers', echoing the eighteenth-century vocabulary of 'drones', updated in the 1980s rhetoric of the idle dependency of the benefits culture.

The unequal regulation, prosecution and sentencing of tax and social security fraud is therefore underpinned by a series of contradictory discourses concerning the status of tax and benefit fraudsters respectively: first, they may be differently regarded as givers to or takers from the state. Second, they may be perceived as the products of the contradictory cultures of enterprise or dependency. Third, they may be regarded as fiddling their own or someone else's money.

Prosecution and punishment: departmental policies

It is impossible to discuss the differential sentencing of tax and social security fraud without first examining the departmental policies which determine both investigatory practice and the official (and effective) rationales behind the decision to prosecute. These policies may involve the use (or misuse) of bargaining and non-prosecution strategies which are, officially, guided by the need to safeguard public funds and maintain departmental integrity, yet are effectively guided by deeper (and contradictory) political and ideological principles. When put into practice, the policies of the Revenue and DSS give rise to very different rates of prosecution, and very different modes of punishment, for the fraudsters involved.

Tax fraud
The Board of Inland Revenue summarizes its current prosecution policy as follows

> While the majority of investigations will lead to a financial settlement, the sanction of criminal prosecution remains for the most serious examples of the various classes of tax fraud. Generally a case will be considered for prosecution if it contains particularly serious features such as forgery or conspiracy, false declarations in investigations or where dishonesty by a tax adviser is involved.
> (Board of Inland Revenue, 1988)

Or, as one tax official succinctly put it to me,

> The first responsibility of the Revenue is to get money in and not to lock people up and prosecute them.

Enforcement policy is thus geared to securing the *compliance* of the taxpayer to the tax laws, and the Revenue regards this as best achieved through negotiation, bargaining and private financial settlement where tax is found to be owed (Keith Committee, 1983). If there is evidence of 'fraud, wilful default or neglect' on the part of a taxpayer, additional financial penalties (and interest on back taxes found to be due) may be imposed. Penalties are calculated as a percentage of tax unpaid and in strict law could be up to 200 per cent, though in practice the Revenue does not seek penalties exceeding 100 per cent (Inland Revenue 1987). This figure is further reduced in accordance with the degree of the taxpayer's co-operation, the gravity of the offence and fullness of voluntary disclosure made. Although compounded financial penalties are presented as a pragmatic response to the aims of collecting taxes, ensuring compliance and deterring tax fraud, they can be used only because tax fraudsters can literally 'pay' for their crimes. By contrast,

Few social security offenders have resources which would make it practicable for the DHSS to apply such a remedy. The result is that, while social security offenders who are prosecuted are publicly identified in the courts and in the media, most tax offenders remain unknown in the community.

(NACRO, 1986b: 89)

Prosecution is reserved only for a selection of the most 'heinous' cases of tax fraud, yet the notion of a general deterrence is invoked in the assertion that 'it is the possibility of prosecution which prevents the spread of tax fraud to unacceptable limits' (NACRO, 1986b: 378). It is a paradox that, on the one hand, Revenue enforcement policy is directed to private financial settlement, yet on the other hand we are asked to believe that the exemplary prosecution of the *very few* (322 convictions in 1987/8) serves as an effective deterrent against fraud, even when the *majority* of fraudsters enjoy negotiated private justice!

Problems also emerge when analysing the practical outcome of Revenue prosecution criteria: the Centre for Policy Studies commented, in evidence to the Keith Committee (on the enforcement powers of the Revenue Departments), that

> ease of presentation of the prosecution case has been a more important factor in the decision to prosecute than it should be. . . . a bigger proportion of the more socially harmful kinds of offences tends to be the subject of negotiated settlement.
>
> (Keith Committee, 1983: 22.1.3)

And so, for instance, it is extremely difficult to prove that a businessman has wilfully understated profits, but relatively easy to prove cases involving the fraudulent misuse of tax exemption certificates (called '714's') in the construction industry, or the theft of Inland Revenue cheques. Consequently of the 322 convictions secured by the Revenue in 1987/8, 170 referred to sub-contractors' exemption certificate frauds and 119 to the theft of Revenue cheques (Board of Inland Revenue, 1988). Only twenty-four related to the submission of false returns of income and accounts – that is, to offences *popularly* regarded as income tax fraud! This disparity does, in part, arise because 'the offences available to the Inland Revenue are ones which require proof of *mens rea* in the form of dishonesty or intent to defraud' (Uglow, 1984: 130).

The offences which *are* prosecuted are thus not only those which are easier to prove, but also the ones which usually equate with what is popularly perceived as 'real crime' (that is akin to theft or forgery) and hence can be easily represented as criminal and as *taking* from the state. By contrast, the understatement of profits is not so readily equated with 'real crime': it may be ambiguously portrayed as merely shrewd or shady business practice (which is difficult to regulate, investigate and effectively sanction) and as, in essence, failing to pay *to* the state and taking from no one. Most of the offences which *are* prosecuted by the Revenue consequently involve 'crime' in the sense of 'taking' (not 'failing to pay') and are investigated by the police or the Board's Investigation Office, which approximates to the Revenue's 'police'. In these respects Revenue prosecution policy is not determined solely by the pragmatic goal of ensuring taxpayers' compliance and the effective collection of taxes: it is also shaped by ideological notions regarding what constitutes acceptable business practice (and acceptable levels of regulation), and by broader stereotypes of real 'crime' and real criminals. Positive images of taxpayers, as entrepreneurial individuals who are the victims of state over-regulation, lie at the heart of the minimal prosecution of those who evade personal taxes.

Supplementary benefit fraud
Throughout the period of intense 'scroungerphobia' in the mid-1970s, DHSS enforcement policy rested on the principle that

> criminal prosecutions should take place . . . wherever the evidence is reasonably adequate to secure a conviction, and that the extenuating circumstances are a matter for the court rather than the prosecutor.
> (Fisher Committee, 1973: 205)

This policy of 'prosecution where appropriate' resulted in criminal proceedings being taken against 20,105 supplementary benefit claimants in 1980/81 (personal communication: DHSS, 1985). But, in accordance with the Thatcher government's emphasis on departmental cost-effectiveness, enforcement policy was reappraised and, following the Rayner team's inquiry in 1980, a 'non-prosecution policy' was adopted. Its aims were reiterated in 1983 (in the wake of the infamous 'Operation Major' anti-fraud swoop against homeless claimants in Oxford) by the then Secretary of State, Hugh Rossi. He stated

> I have taken the view that it is far more important and humane to check the abuse of the system when it is detected and to try to recover the money than to mount expensive prosecutions and to drag those individuals through the courts.
> (*Hansard*, 7 February 1983, col. 811)

On the face of it this non-prosecution policy is to be welcomed as it has certainly led to a reduction in claimants brought before the courts: in 1985/6 there were 8,902 supplementary benefit prosecutions compared with over 20,000 five years previously (personal communication: DHSS, 1988). But in practical terms the policy has several worrying aspects. First, the non-prosecution interview is geared to achieving 'benefit savings' by encouraging claimants suspected of fraud to withdraw their claim. Critics have argued that the Special Claims Control Units (SCCUs) set up in 1981 to spearhead this policy may have coerced claimants into forfeiting their claim to benefit in circumstances where there was insufficient evidence of fraud, and where a prosecution would certainly have failed (P. Moore, 1981; CPSA, 1984). Equally the *modus operandi* of SCCUs have been seen to involve intimidation,

> questionable interrogation techniques and unacceptable pressure to produce benefit savings, all in an atmosphere overcharged with the desire to meet targetted savings and root out fraud.
>
> (R. Smith, 1985: 118)

Mr Rossi's view of a 'humane' non-prosecution strategy is therefore highly questionable both in theory and in practice because cutting costs (incurred by prosecution itself), recovering money through benefit 'savings' and punishing 'scroungers' are the effective rationales underpinning DHSS enforcement policy in the 1980s. Consequently 'humanity' features in political rhetoric rather than in the practices of those handling cases of suspected fraud (Cook 1989; NACRO, 1986b; R. Smith, 1985; Beltram, 1984).

The key aims and methods of the DSS's current enforcement policy were amply demonstrated in television coverage showing examples of a non-prosecution strategy in action against unemployed claimants suspected of fraud. According to a Department of Employment official, the BBC *40 Minutes* programme *Dolebusters* (screened in October 1988) was 'a good picture of the work this team does' (*Tempo*, 1988). The investigations it screened were either based on anonymous tip-offs from members of the public, or adopted a proactive approach: targeting fraud-prone jobs (in, for instance, the building trade and taxi firms), the surveillance of claimants' vehicles for signs of work (tools, a bucket, a ladder . . .) or the scrutiny of the claimants themselves for 'dirty hands' (BBC, *Dolebusters*, October 1988). It is inconceivable that the great British taxpayer would be physically scrutinized and accused of fraud on the basis of clothing that was adjudged too smart for their declared salary level, yet this is the kind of intrusive regulation which is justified where the suspect is perceived as a *taker* from the public purse.

Also evident through this programme was the gross inequality in the respective rights of claimant and taxpayer accused of fraud: a taxpayer so accused would be encouraged to have a legal adviser present at interviews with Revenue staff, and interviews would be conducted in a manner reflecting departmental emphasis on the *rights* of the taxpayer (*Taxpayers' Charter*, 1986). By contrast, *Dolebusters* showed an unemployed man interviewed, under caution, in the back seat of an investigator's car, being told of his right to seek legal advice – a totally meaningless 'right' given the conditions of the interview.

Regardless of the merits or otherwise of any single case, what is at issue here is the morality of a non-prosecution policy which encourages claimants to withdraw their benefit claims 'or else'. First, the alleged 'evidence' on which they are so advised may be a malicious letter, anonymous telephone call or the fact that the claimant drives a van which contains a bucket! Clearly such evidence would be insufficient to mount a prosecution, yet is often used to 'persuade' claimants to 'sign off'. Second, claimants are thus 'paying' for alleged crimes (without being convicted), by forfeiting their entitlement to state benefits. The result may be 'benefit savings' for the Treasury, but it cannot be considered justice. In the words of one magistrate, the non-prosecution interview 'seems to have some elements of blackmail'. Third, the 'or else' alternative – the threat of prosecution – was *still* applied to over 9,000 supplementary benefit claimants in 1987/8, making a nonsense of the apparent policy rationales of 'humanity' and the desire not to 'drag individuals through the courts'. The outcome of a non-prosecution strategy is very different when applied to taxpayers who have failed to declare income: for them non-prosecution, financial penalty and private justice have positive advantages.

Paying the penalty

It is often alleged that tax fraudsters have already 'paid' for their offences, by repayment of taxes due and sometimes by additional financial penalty, and that prosecution would be both gratuitous and counter-productive. For this reason the taxpayer's ability to pay is in effect offered as a justification for an enforcement policy which 'spares the taxpayer's feelings' (Keith Committee 1983). But, at the same time, it is also argued that financial penalties *are* a form of punishment on a par with the punishments available under the criminal justice system: for instance, one accountant (also a magistrate) commented that a financial penalty was 'in effect a fine'. Another accountant/magistrate felt that penalties were an effective deterrent because 'very few people will offend twice'. Clearly then, there is a belief that individuals who repay evaded taxes have made reparation, and that if additional financial penalties are imposed, they have been *punished* too. Penalties are also justified as a practical means of fulfilling the Revenue's primary function – collecting tax – because *private* negotiations facilitate full disclosure and speedy settlement. But one senior Revenue official felt that although compliance may well be encouraged by settling 'out of court, as it were', there was a need to

> weigh up the relative value of publicity as a deterrent in relation to *lack* of publicity being helpful in a handful of cases.

He noted that 'publicity usually surrounds the "have-nots" getting caned, not the higher income groups'.

As already argued, taxpayers are in a position to be able to offer to 'pay for their crimes; benefit claimants are not. None the less, it should be stressed that wherever benefits are overpaid (for reasons other than 'official error'), claimants *are* required to pay (NACRO, 1986b). Current regulations state that where a claimant admits fraud, up to £6.80 per week may be deducted from future benefit payments until the debt to the DSS has been repaid (CPAG, 1988). It is difficult to see how benefit fraud is deterred by enforcement policies which may reduce a claimant's income to £6.80 below the poverty line and, if criminal proceedings are then taken, may possibly reduce that income still further through a fine. Ironically in such circumstances, fraud may become the only means of economic survival for some benefit claimants.

To summarize, there are several paradoxes within official discourses on Revenue and DSS enforcement policy. Both departments stress cost-effectiveness, the importance of safeguarding public funds and espouse non-prosecution policies. Yet in 1987/8 these policies resulted in only 322 Revenue prosecutions compared with 9,847 for supplementary benefit fraud (personal communication, DHSS, 1988; Board of Inland Revenue, 1988). In the same year the total yield from the Revenue's *compliance* activities was £2,013 million (Board of Inland Revenue, 1988), yet when Norman Fowler spoke of 'taxpayer's money being used to finance the fraudulent' (*Guardian*, 13 October 1988) he was speaking about unemployed benefit claimants who work on the side, not about the far more costly fiddles of the taxpayers themselves! More manpower and resources are directed against 'scroungers' than tax evaders despite the fact that tax fraud is of far greater magnitude (NACRO, 1986b; HC 102, 1983/4; Keith Committee 1983: 772). The official rhetoric of 'cost-effectiveness' and 'benefit savings' is therefore put into practice very selectively. As a result most taxpayers pay for defrauding the public purse through private financial settlement, yet thousands of benefit claimants each year pay twice – through reparation to the DSS and through sentences imposed by the courts.

Sentencing: the data

Having established that very few tax fraudsters are prosecuted, and that those who are prosecuted have often committed offences akin to theft (for instance, of Revenue cheques) and forgery (misuse of 714 exemption certificates), it follows that any analysis of the sentencing of tax evaders will be based on a very small number of cases. By contrast, there are thousands of prosecutions each year for supplementary benefit (now income support) fraud. But several difficulties arise when attempting to make sentencing comparisons as the relevant data are not comprehensive or complete. For instance, first, the Revenue and DSS do not publish information on sentencing, as this is seen to be the responsibility of the courts. Second, the

Home Office statistics, based on categories such as 'Revenue Law offences' and 'Social Security offences', make it impossible to distinguish, for instance, those tax and supplementary benefit fraudsters who have been prosecuted under other categories, such as the Theft Act. Third, the use of overall categories such as 'Social Security offence' conceals distinctions between contributory and non-contributory (means-tested) benefits. As a result, it is impossible to tell what benefit has been fiddled!

Despite many practical difficulties in obtaining precise comparable data, a NACRO Working Party reporting on *Enforcement of the Law Relating to Social Security* (1986b) did make specific comparisons with the enforcement of Revenue Laws. Evidence to the working party had stressed the use of 'harsher penalties against social security offences than against those infringing tax laws'. In relation to prosecutions mounted, the ratio of prosecutions brought for Revenue and Social Security offences respectively, was around 1:30 in 1984 (NACRO, 1986b: 69). Moreover, the report noted 'the relative severity of the custodial sentences in some cases, compared with sentences for comparably serious offences in spheres other than social security'. This observation was supported by unpublished DHSS figures which indicated that in 1984/5 433 unsuspended prison sentences were imposed for benefit frauds in England, Wales and Scotland (NACRO, 1986b: 76–7). The report concluded that

> Sometimes . . . the sentencing authority is influenced by the tendency . . . to attach a special kind of moral turpitude to people living on benefits.
>
> (NACRO, 1986b: 77)

This is certainly true of many of the sentencing discourses which will be discussed below.

The analysis which follows will be based upon official commentaries on criminal proceedings mounted by the Inland Revenue from 1982 to 1988,[3] details of 206 cases of supplementary benefit fraud heard in one magistrates' court in the Midlands from 1981 to 1987,[4] and media coverage of tax and supplementary benefit fraud cases. In relation to the latter, publicity is inextricably linked to the reporting of criminal proceedings in the courts, and if tax fraud cases do not reach the courts, then public awareness of the extent and costs of tax evasion will be minimal. By contrast, local newspapers reporting proceedings in magistrates' courts will cover many 'scrounger' stories, thereby reinforcing the belief that benefit fraud is the more widespread and poses the greater threat to the 'taxpayer' and hence to society. The media, therefore, not only reproduce the sentencing discourses of the courts, but also produce the ideological conditions and the vocabularies within which such discourses are sustained and justified (Golding and Middleton, 1982).

Sentencing: tax fraud

In July 1986 an unqualified accountant who, over a seven-year period, had concealed income amounting to £98,000 from the Inland Revenue, was reminded by the judge sentencing him that the Court of Appeal had ruled that those guilty of persistent dishonesty must expect a custodial sentence and a financial penalty. The accountant was sentenced to four months' imprisonment and fined £10,000 (personal communication, Association of Inspectors of Taxes (AIT), 1988). In June 1987 the joint owner of an Italian restaurant was sentenced to nine months' imprisonment for a £176,000 tax fraud. The judge commented that the defendants had engaged in 'a highly unsocial activity which worked to the disadvantage of all honest taxpayers and continued that 'the Courts have shown that immediate custodial sentences are required except in exceptional circumstances' (ibid).

On the face ot it, then, the sentencing of tax fraudsters should reflect the degree of economic and social harm the offences inflict on society and, if a persistent fraud is involved should result in financial penalty in addition to custody. However, in practice there are a variety of circumstances relating to the status of the offender and the extent of his/her admission of guilt which distorts the sentencing process. For instance, the restaurateur mentioned above had made a false declaration of 'full disclosure' following an earlier investigation in 1984. His failure to admit at the outset the full extent of his concealed income was an important factor affecting his relatively severe sentence. By contrast, two wholesale market traders who defrauded over £12,000 were fined £5,000 because they were first offenders, had made restitution to the Revenue and had co-operated with the investigation (ibid.). (But, as will be argued below, where supplementary benefit fraud is concerned, almost all offenders plead guilty, all are required to make restitution to the DSS, yet this does not similarly mitigate their sentences.)

In the case of Lester Piggott, Judge Farquason commented that if Piggott had fully disclosed details of his income to the Revenue, he might have found it possible to be 'lenient' with him (ibid.). This is remarkable in view of the scale of Piggott's offences (tax and interest in excess of £3 million owed) and their persistence (since initial investigations in 1981), yet demonstrates that even when tax fraudsters are recidivists, their offences may be largely mitigated by full admission of guilt and paying back the taxes defrauded. Mitigation may also arise from the 'status' of the offender himself, although in Piggott's case the vast amount he defrauded (and his failure to 'come clean' to the Revenue earlier) effectively ruled out any such mitigation for the 'housewives' choice' jockey. He was sentenced to three years in custody. However, others have successfully used their status in the community as mitigation: for example, the director of a dispensing chemists (who was also a Justice of the Peace!) was found guilty of submitting false trading accounts. Although over £28,000 had been defrauded, defence counsel argued against a custodial sentence on the grounds that the director had paid back taxes owing, admitted his guilt and had served the community as a JP and a worker for charity. The judge took such 'work for the community' into account when suspending the nine months' custodial sentence, but ironically pointed out that 'tax evasion is effectively stealing from the community' (personal communication, AIT, 1988).

In a similar vein, it was pleaded that a chartered accountant, prosecuted in 1982 for falsifying accounts, 'had been a busy professional man, of high reputation in the community, who had now lost everything'. Clearly the magistrates who sentenced him to fines of £1,500 accepted that his 'career had been shattered' and that he had, in effect, already been punished through the social stigma of criminal proceedings (ibid.). This theme is found in the subsequent sentencing of many other tax fraudsters where, for instance, 'anxiety and general disgrace' or 'previous good character' is seen to justify a fine. But, in turn, the fine is seen as an available penalty because tax fraudsters can usually 'pay' for their crimes by this means. The notion that to come from a 'good' social background is in itself mitigation (because such offenders are seen to suffer loss of status through prosecution itself) is also evident in the case of two directors of an engineering company, who in 1983 had been found guilty of a £40,000 tax fraud. They were sentenced to pay £5,000 fines and their six months' custodial sentences were suspended, as the judge commented it was 'sad to see men of their background' involved in a persistent and substantial Revenue fraud (ibid.).

But some tax fraudsters may benefit from their relatively high social status and, where applicable, from their lack of financial means too: for instance, a partner in a firm of accountants who illegally transferred funds to offshore companies to evade UK taxes was given a nine months' suspended sentence because of his professional inexperience and the professional ruin which would follow the case. Yet the judge also accepted that the offender was 'virtually penniless' and so did not impose a fine or costs! (ibid.). By comparison, *all* benefit fraudsters suffer from being 'penniless', but this certainly does not exempt them from paying either fines or costs. But, as already argued, the taxpayer is regarded by definition a giver to the state, assumed to be guided by positive entrepreneurial values and to be essentially 'non-criminal' in terms of personal and social characteristics. These assumptions underpin both the minimal use of criminal sanction against tax fraudsters and the often compassionate views of sentencers.

Sentencing supplementary benefit fraud

In March 1987 Lord Lane heard six appeals from social security fraud offenders sentenced to over one year in custody, one of whom had been gaoled for thirty months! He said that

It is clear that in order to qualify for prosecution at all, offences must
be other than minor.

(*Guardian*, 25 March 1987)

He accordingly reduced their sentences to between four and six months. But
at the same time he dismissed other appeals by three 'drifters' who had used
false names to fiddle the DHSS: their custodial sentences, of three to four
years, were upheld. Even though it could be argued that such itinerant frauds
are premeditated and that these offenders 'make a business out of cheating
the public purse', it is difficult to justify sentences of three to four years while
those who make far more money at this 'business' (through tax fraud) are
sentenced so leniently.

In urging judges to reduce prison sentences for social security offences
Lord Lane argued that the element of 'deterrence' should not play a large part
in the sentencing of such cases (ibid.). But the magistrates who sentence the
vast majority of benefit fraudsters clearly think (and act) differently.
Magistrates I have spoken to see deterrence as the primary reason for
prosecution (a view echoed by some DHSS staff), but paradoxically one
magistrate still felt that 'It is true to say that we sometimes feel the offence to
have been trivial'. Another was under the misapprehension that the DHSS
'wouldn't probably prosecute if the claimant "coughed" at the interview
stage'. As the following observations of the sentencing of supplementary
benefit fraud indicate, the admission of guilt and the scale of the fraud cannot
account for the inconsistent (and contradictory) sentencing rationales
invoked for social security offenders.

First, to take the issue of guilt: of the 206 cases of supplementary benefit
fraud I have analysed, 191 (93 per cent) pleaded guilty and hence the
conviction rate was very high, with 201 claimants found guilty. Some
claimants are totally unprepared for the court proceedings which may follow
their admission of guilt: for instance, Barry had admitted doing casual work
'on the side' when he was visited by a DHSS official, but was unrepresented
in the magistrates' court, as were 43 per cent of my sample. (He had been told
that the case was unlikely to go to court!) It seems that the admission of guilt
plays no part in the DHSS decision to prosecute: such decisions are made
locally with a good deal of managerial discretion (NACRO, 1986b). This
may influence the second issue – the seriousness (or triviality) of cases
brought before the courts.

Lord Lane indicated that offences prosecuted 'must be other than trivial'
(*Guardian*, 25 March 1987): official guidelines suggested that a minimum of
£250 should have been defrauded. This figure seems extremely low in
relation to the scale which tax frauds have to reach in order to attract
prosecution but, even then, this minimum does not apply to fiddles involving
the alteration, theft or misuse of girocheques (ibid.). In practice, this means
that supplementary benefit claimants may be prosecuted for fiddling giros
worth less than, for example, the £70 which the Inland Revenue write-off as

'not worth recovery' from PAYE taxpayers. The scale of the fiddle does not always determine sentencing in such cases: for instance, four of the six immediate custodial sentences passed in one Midlands magistrates' court over my period of research (referred to in Table 6.1) were imposed for giro frauds. In one case the amount defrauded was only £67.10. Three suspended prison sentences were imposed for giro fiddles worth £63, £94 and £129 respectively. It is inconceivable that tax evasion resulting in losses to the Revenue of such small amounts would be considered worthy of prosecution, let alone a custodial sentence. Such sentences also belie the assumption that only 'serious' cases of benefit fraud are prosecuted. Although many giro frauds are considered closest to 'crime' in the sense that some involve forgery or theft, they are usually desperately crass frauds motivated by poverty, rather than organized frauds motivated by greed (Cook, 1989).

All supplementary benefit fraudsters I spoke to justified their crimes as their only available response to the situation of hopelessness, chronic poverty and degradation in which they found themselves (see Chapter 1 in this volume). Yet these justifications are not ones which can be successfully invoked in court. One magistrate I spoke to summarized a common view amongst sentencers: 'I don't want excuses', he said, and argued that offenders would do better to admit they are wrong and 'say sorry'. But this view may lead to harsh reactions towards those who do not (or cannot) play the game as magistrates wish. For example, Bert had worked 'on the side' as a building-site labourer while claiming benefit and was repaying the £572 he owed to the DHSS. Several factors may have been offered as mitigation: Bert told me that he had recently been separated from his wife and was attempting to 'set up home again'. He had difficulty paying for household goods and clothes, and still wanted to buy presents for his children. But when magistrates asked him if he had anything to say before sentence, Bert (who was unrepresented) shrugged his shoulders and said, 'It was one of those things, I suppose'. Not only were the magistrates unaware of his personal circumstances, but also they showed great displeasure at what they considered to be his flippant attitude, though like many poorer defendants, he was nervous and confused by the proceedings (Carlen, 1976; Crow and Simon, 1987). He was sentenced to pay fines of £180 (and costs).

As most benefit frauds are motivated by poverty, it is particularly inappropriate that the fine remains the most popular sentence for benefit fraud (Table 6.1). Despite a decline in the overall use of the fine as mass unemployment became a fact of economic and social life in the 1980s, NACRO found that courts were reluctant to modify their use of financial penalties in cases of social security fraud (Crow and Simon, 1987: 48).

The practical effects of imposing fines upon those least able to pay them was well demonstrated in the case of Jim, a father of three young children, who was prosecuted in 1986 for failing to declare his wife's part-time earnings. He had been overpaid £996 in benefits and this was being repaid to the DHSS by deductions of £1.65 per week from his supplementary

Table 6.1 The sentencing of 206 supplementary benefit fraud cases in one
Midlands magistrates' court October 1981 to August 1987

Sentence passed	Number of cases	(%)
Immediate custodial sentence	6	3.0
Suspended custodial sentence	11	5.4
Community service order	22	10.9
Probation order	26	12.9
Fine	82	40.8
Conditional discharge	54	27.0
Total	201	100.0

Note: Costs awarded to the DHSS in 156 cases (78 per cent).

benefit (as it had been agreed he could repay no more than this weekly
amount). He had accumulated debts exceeding £1,000 arising from loans,
clothing clubs and hire purchase payments and had seen his wife's earnings
as a way of paying off these debts. Ironically magistrates sentenced him to
pay fines totalling £210 (and costs!), at the rate of £3 per week and
commented that

> This country is fed up to the teeth with people like you scrounging from
> your fellow citizens.

Moreover, benefit fraud was said to be 'one of the worst forms of stealing
there is'. Privately, Jim's response to the sentence was to say that the
magistrate was 'on another planet to us' and, despairingly, he joked that

> Ah well, it's the red light under the porch now.

It is difficult to envisage any legal means by which he *could* pay such fines.

   Jim's case is not untypical: most of the benefit fraudsters I observed in
court were in debt and found it impossible to make repayment of loans on
low and fixed levels of supplementary benefit. (Following the April 1988
changes which introduced income support and state-sponsored loans
through the Social Fund, it is likely that the material conditions of poverty
and debt which generate fraud are worsening for many claimants.)
   In another case, Jeff (a father of three) had recently been made redundant
and his wife had taken a part-time cleaning job to clear debts (for 'clothing
clubs' and the purchase of a washing machine). Her earnings had totalled
£280 and at the time of the hearing this amount was being repaid to the
DHSS by deductions of £3 per week from his supplementary benefit. Jeff and
his wife were anxious and upset about the court case: they were first
offenders. The magistrate, however, considered Jeff's 'taking from the state'

as very serious because 'rules are to be kept' and imposed fines totalling £100 (and costs). It could be argued that the fines, to be repaid at the rate of £2 per week from benefits that were already £3 lower than the basic supplementary benefit level (because of repayment direct to the DHSS) were a very harsh sentence: guilt had been readily admitted, compensation was being paid, and the experience of being taken to court had already proved a harsh deterrent for Jeff and his wife. When compared to the negotiated private justice enjoyed by those who 'take from the state' through tax evasion, the sentence seems still less appropriate.

Although not demonstrated in Table 6.1, there has recently been a decline in the use of the fine for supplementary benefit offenders in the Midlands area I studied: for example, of those sentenced there between 1981 and 1983, 48 per cent were fined. But by 1986/7 this figure had fallen to 37 per cent, accompanied by an *increase* in the use of the conditional discharge. While this sentencing trend is to be welcomed, it does raise questions about the DHSS's prosecution policy. As NACRO has pointed out,

> The process of investigation, formal warning of the consequences of a further offence and recovery of the amount overpaid will usually be sufficient to chasten and deter.
>
> (NACRO, 1986b: 73)

If this is the case, prosecution (even if it results in a conditional discharge) can be seen as gratuitous. A fine can be seen as entirely counter-productive.

There is much inconsistency regarding what constitutes appropriate 'deterrence' for those who defraud the public purse. Tax evasion is seen as best deterred in part by the exemplary prosecution of a very few of the worst cases of tax 'crime', but largely by individuals' making private settlements with the Revenue (lack of publicity facilitating compliance to this end). Benefit fraud is seen as deterred through the fairly arbitrary prosecution of those whom local DHSS officials deem 'serious' fraudsters, with maximum publicity being sought. Yet DHSS staff, prosecuting solicitors and some magistrates *privately* admit that for benefit fraudsters such deterrence is ineffective. None the less, they justify both prosecution and (relatively harsh) sentences by the ritual invocation 'Well, you have to do *something* with them'. But this futile justification is not required for the majority of tax fraudsters who never appear in the courts: it seems that *nothing* needs to be done with them. Those who *do* appear in the courts do not attract the public villification that is reserved for the poor who defraud the public purse (Golding and Middleton, 1982). They are also well able to pay for their crimes by financial penalties and by loss of their social status – status which the poor do not possess and so cannot lose.

Doing something about the unequal punishment of tax and benefit fraud

In conclusion, I would argue that we *can* do something to reduce the injustices described here. First, more manpower and resources could be directed to the investigation and regulation of tax evasion. Currently, counter-evasion officers working in local tax offices yield fifteen times their own salaries in taxes recouped, and officers in Special Offices yield thirty-two times their salaries (Board of Inland Revenue 1988: 41). On grounds of cost-effectiveness alone, the government should be pressured to recruit more staff to regulate tax evasion than social security fraud. Second, on grounds of consistency and social justice, the prosecution polices of the DSS and Inland Revenue should be reviewed. If the DSS is really *serious* about its non-prosecution policy, then the claimant's rights should be safeguarded during 'non-prosecution interviews', and the number of prosecutions mounted by the DSS should still be greatly reduced. At the same time, the Revenue should consider the deterrent value of, first, mounting so few (and so selective) prosecutions, and second, of private financial settlements. The Keith Committee Report (1983) suggested that the names of tax defaulters should be published as a deterrent to fraud, a possibility which was again raised by NACRO (1986b). The Revenue remain squeamish about publishing the names of those individuals who are usually, after all, 'good upstanding citizens'! None the less, research has indicated that tax fraudsters are *more* likely to be deterred by the threat of adverse publicity than private settlement or, indeed, certain criminal sanctions: for instance, in a questionnaire survey of fifty-six executives, 'national publicity' of their offending was regarded as a more severe penalty than the imposition of either a £5,000 fine or a two-year suspended prison sentence (Levi, 1987: 321)! The option of deterrent publicity is one which could very easily be taken up, and which would stigmatize (and inflict an effective punishment on) tax evaders, without further increasing the prison population.

Social security fraud is one of the least deterrable crimes because it is generated by poverty. Tax evasion is, in theory, a very deterrable crime because it is motivated not by need but by greed. This simple observation is obscured by the historical legacy of imagery about the idle poor and the energetic, thrifty taxpayer, updated in the rhetoric of the enterprise and benefit cultures. Currently the poor 'pay' more, and more often, for defrauding the state than do the rich whose fiddles are far more costly. It is ironic that common-sense critiques of allegedly lenient sentences of poorer offenders often argue that poverty appears to license crime (see Chapter 1 in this volume). But, on the evidence of this chapter, I would argue that the reverse is true: poverty itself inculpates the poor, while wealth and 'enterprise' exculpates the rich.

Notes

1 The research on which most of this chapter is based was conducted before April

1988, and so the term 'supplementary benefit' will continue to be used wherever applicable. Income support, which replaced supplementary benefit following the April reforms, will be referred to only when discussing current enforcement policies or administrative regulations which differ from those in force at the time of my research. Also, since mid 1988, the social services department is DSS not DHSS.

2 The research which forms the core of this chapter aimed to compare the commission, regulation, investigation and punishment of supplementary benefit fraud and income tax fraud: the latter was restricted to enable a meaningful comparison between the experiences of *individual* claimants and taxpayers. For this reason large-scale corporate tax frauds are not dealt with here.

3 The Inland Revenue Staff Federation and Association of Inspectors of Taxes kindly provided me with details of prosecution policy and official commentaries on criminal proceedings. Although this information was already 'in the public domain', thanks are due to them for making the task of research easier for me.

4 Details of a sample of 206 supplementary benefit fraud cases heard in one magistrates' court in the Midlands refer to a period between 1981 and 1987. Information was collected on pleas, verdicts, representation, sentencing and the award of costs and compensation. In addition court proceedings were observed in several cases of benefit fraud and, wherever practical, I spoke to the fraudsters involved.

7
Alternatives to and in prisons: a realist approach

Roger Matthews

Introduction

By the end of the century the number of people in prison could be halved. The means for achieving this goal are already available and it is an objective which is gathering political momentum. The main obstacle appears to lie in devising and implementing an effective reform strategy.

But even realizing the objective – which is a difficult enough task in itself – is not sufficient, for the crisis currently facing the prisons is not merely one of overcrowding and the deteriorating penal conditions which invariably accompany it. Overcrowding is only the most immediate representation of a much more fundamental crisis – a crisis of legitimacy. Overcrowding no doubt exacerbates existing problems, but its removal would still leave unanswered the question of who should go to prison, for how long and for what purpose. It would also leave open questions about the organization and the proper role of the prison. And, most importantly, it would leave untouched the central question of the proper relation between the prison and the community which it is supposed to serve.

The deepening penal crisis is increasingly being reinforced by a growing disillusionment about the viability of community-based corrections. The criticisms which were once laid at the door of the prison are now being directed towards the expanding forms of community-based 'alternatives' to custody. They have, it is claimed, failed to live up to their original promises (Austin and Krisberg, 1982). Instead, they have served inadvertently to expand the penal sphere by drawing into the criminal justice system an ever-larger population – a predictable percentage of whom will eventually end up in prison. This has led to the bizarre situation in which the community-based alternatives are depicted as being more of a problem than a solution and in which the prison and the so-called alternatives reinforce each other through their persistent and implacable 'failures'. In consequence there has emerged a parallel crisis in which both the prison and community-based facilities are charged either with not being corrective enough or with being insufficiently reformative. Against the background of this apparent impasse the re-expansion of the prison is now being promoted as the only politically viable response to overcrowding and the 'rising tide of crime' (Matthews, 1987a).

It is, however, paradoxical that the new prison-building programmes are occurring against a background of mounting criticism of the prison system from right across the political spectrum. Even those who pursue expansionist penal programmes tend to do so apologetically. Nevertheless, expansionism is clearly back on the agenda – and even in countries which less than a decade ago were noted for their decarceration policies (Downes, 1988; De Haan, 1986; Hulsman, 1982; Morrison, 1985). As expansionism becomes more extensive the debate has increasingly focused on the question of whether penal institutions ought to be 'public' or 'private' (Ericson *et al.*, 1987; Borna, 1986; Ryan and Ward, 1989). The debate around 'privatization' is not insignificant but it does not directly address the crucial question of how the apparently inexorable drive towards prison expansion can be arrested and how a more constructive and appropriate set of responses can be implemented.

Given the significant level of political support which has been repeatedly expressed for reducing the custodial population and, given too, the array of policies which have been developed to try to minimize the use of imprisonment one can only conclude that there must be serious limitations in either the design or the implementation of these reforms. Some have been imaginative and innovative; within certain parameters, gains have been made – often under adverse economic and political conditions. But substantive long-term improvements are disappointingly few and far between and there is a growing sense that more radical but realistic policies are needed.

Clearly, if we are to move beyond the current impasse and the prevailing mood of pessimism there is a pressing need to re-examine the process of penal reform and to develop strategies which can overcome the recognized pitfalls. Much of the recent debate has, however, centred around approaches which are overly negative, idealistic or administrative. These approaches are becoming increasingly sceptical about the possibilities of implementing effective reforms at all.

A realist approach sets itself against these tendencies and argues that the variability in the level of incarceration and in the nature of penal conditions in different countries itself suggests that there is considerable scope for reform – particularly in countries like Britain and the USA which score high on the scale of the number of people per 100,000 which they incarcerate and score relatively low on the scale of prison conditions and organization (Van Dijk, 1988; Rutherford, 1984; Stern, 1987).

A realistic approach also begins from the premise that there is no invariable relationship between the rates of recorded crime and the level of imprisonment (see Chapter 1 in this volume); although unlike some 'idealists' it does not move to the other extreme and claim that the level of imprisonment is totally unrelated to the incidence of crime. In fact, a central concern of realism is to re-examine critically the relationship between crime and imprisonment and to foster a more reflexive relation between them (see Matthews, 1987b; J. Young, 1989).

In the post-war period the prison has increasingly become an institution of containment rather than retribution. At the same time it has become less of a mechanism for disciplining labour and more one for warehousing the unemployed and the unemployables. Thus:

> A realistic reading of penal statistics – in terms of processes and not just products – shows that the prison service operates more as a system of managing 'bad risks' than as an extended and systematic theory of management of illegal behaviour by the proletariat.
>
> (Faugeron and Houchon, 1987; 396)

The development of a viable penal strategy must reflect some understanding of the social composition of penal populations. They are composed largely of the poor, the disaffected, the marginalized, the 'expelled' and the destitute (Mathieson, 1974). For much working-class illegality – particularly occupational illegality – like much 'white-collar' crime receives relatively little formal attention. The regulation of the 'hidden economy' generally elicits a more informal and less stigmatizing response (Henry, 1983; South and Scraton, 1981). That is, it is in relation to the actual composition of the custodial population that reform strategies need to be developed, and that the abstract justifications for punishment – retribution, deterrence, reform and incapacitation – need to be considered.

There is a pressing need to reconsider the general processes of reform. Criminologists and penologists have not given this question too much serious attention. Instead, they tend to offer 'quick fit' or 'one off' solutions' which more often than not fall short of the desired objectives.

Taking penal reform seriously

Radical realism is principally concerned with developing and implementing effective reforms. The formulation and implementation of reforms have been surrounded by a series of recurring problems (Brown, 1987; Fattah, 1987). Radicals in particular have posed the question of how to frame reforms which do not continually produce unanticipated and undesirable effects, and which are not co-opted in the process of implementation.

Thomas Mathieson's widely critiqued answer to this question involved making a distinction between 'positive' and 'negative' reforms (Mathieson, 1974). In seeking to avoid the revolution/reform dichotomy and to promote a more open-ended and fluid strategy he emphasized the notion of 'the unfinished'. Mathieson sought to distinguish between piecemeal liberal reforms which, however well intentioned, succeeded only in reinforcing the existing penal system and those interventions which undermined it. 'Positive' reforms which do not challenge the existing system are to be avoided and replaced by a series of 'negative' reforms which actively confront existing arrangements.

Mathieson's critique of liberal reformism is well founded but his distinction between 'positive' and 'negative' reforms is not only difficult to sustain in practice but also can act as an impediment to transforming existing penal institutions (Greenberg, 1983). The aim of improving prison conditions, for example, is treated by Mathieson and other abolitionists with ambivalence since it constitutes a positive reform. Similarly the notion of the 'unfinished' presents difficulties in developing a progressive penal policy. The reluctance which abolitionists express towards spelling out objectives may help to avoid the problem of co-option but does not help in the process of mobilizing social and political support. As David Downes has argued:

> Either the 'unfinished' means little more than being pragmatic and flexible (which does not rule out resistance to incorporation, the pursuit of abolition; and the alliance with the 'expelled') or it implies working to bring about a society where one is not allowed to theorise. Suppose one *had* an alternative; should one keep quiet about it? Mathieson seems to invoke a species of guilt-by-association in his attitude towards alternatives. Because the system makes a great deal of the need to specify them as a delaying tactic, therefore they become a bad thing in themselves. Ultimately, the 'unfinished' can become the nebulous in a profoundly anti-democratic way, since alternatives are never formulated clearly enough for people to make rational choices between them.
>
> (Downes, 1980: 82)

All reformers tend to describe their own programmes as 'progressive'. But how one defines 'progressive' will depend upon the particular political orientation of the reformer and this in turn will be linked to the vision of the future. In this sense all reform strategies are utopian – since they are yet-to-be-realized. There is no contradiction between 'visionary' and 'practical' politics. What distinguishes a realist approach from that of other radicals like Mathieson is that it is concerned with constructing an agenda around which rational discussion can take place. The notion of a rational discussion is premised upon the realization of an open and democratic framework for debate. For radical realists the basic commitment to democratization also involves an emphasis upon accountability, the provision of a plurality of decision-making sites, the formulation of more responsive and appropriate institutions, and the matching of social need and social provision (Lea and Young, 1984).

There is no formal contradiction between the pursuit of these objectives and the development of a cost-effective criminal justice system. On the contrary, some combinations of them may be necessary prerequisites for developing a more efficient and responsive system (see Kinsey *et al.*, 1986). Most of these objectives it has been repeatedly pointed out have a low priority in the penal sphere, which for the most part is characterized by inertia, secrecy and inefficiency.

Overcoming the limitations requires the formulation of an effective reform strategy. At the most general level there is a choice between abolishing or dismantling the institutions themselves – 'deep end' strategies – or of reducing the intake of offenders into prison – 'shallow end' strategies.

'Deep end' and 'shallow end' strategies

The growth of the abolitionist movement in the 1970s encouraged the prioritization of 'deep end' strategies aimed at closing down penal institutions. There have been, however, very few attempts to date actually to close down penal institutions and most 'second generation' abolitionists and other penal reformers have increasingly come to focus upon limiting prison capacity or preventing the expansion of the existing penal network (Mathieson, 1986).

The main reference point for the possibility of closing down institutions remains the so-called Massachusetts Experiment (Bakal and Polsky, 1978). This initiative – which is credited with closing down the juvenile reformatories in Massachusetts 'virtually overnight' – is widely seen as the consummate example of how radical decarceration can be realized. However, its significance has been overplayed. For although it serves as a constant reminder that a significant degree of decarceration can be achieved without causing massive social problems and without fuelling the growth of crime it remains a very 'idiosyncratic' experiment which was achievable only as a result of the particular political configurations in Massachusetts which allowed the entrepreneurial abilities of Jerry Miller, who was at the time the commissioner of the newly constituted Department of Youth Services, to flourish.

Because of these unique circumstances the Massachusetts Experiment was unable to provide any model of reform. Not surprisingly therefore this apparently 'successful' strategy did not set in motion a series of similar 'experiments' across the country. Neither was it the outcome of any democratic processes. Rather it was achieved 'by sidestepping bureaucratic obstacles' (Rutherford, 1986). Nor, apparently, did it reduce the level of recidivism or decrease costs (Serrill, 1975). Instead it fed into the expanding privatized network of juvenile control which in turn created a more opaque and less accountable system of juvenile justice (Lerman, 1984; Schwartz *et al.*, 1986).

The difficulties of duplicating this kind of initiative has led to a shift of emphasis in most 'deep end' reformers towards limiting penal capacity and to declaring a moratorium on prison construction (Nagel, 1977; Blumstein, 1987). This policy, too, is not without serious limitations. In its simplest form it claims that the non-availability of prison places will provide a disincentive to the judiciary to give custodial dispositions above a certain level. However, in a number of countries we have seen that the lack of available prison places does not dissuade members of the judiciary from giving custodial sentences; rather it seems to have produced ever higher levels of overcrowding. In England and Wales the response to the lack of available places in prisons has resulted in over 1,000 people being kept nightly in police cells. Thus, on its own this basic strategy could lead to a worsening of prison conditions and further overcrowding. Unless there are simultaneous restrictions on the number of persons per cell and agreed minimum conditions of confinement, a reduction of prison places is likely to aggravate rather than resolve the present crisis. However, even where minimum conditions are enforced this approach can lead to the type of waiting system which was adopted in the Netherlands in which convicted offenders take up prison places only as and when they become available. This introduces a system which not only potentially undermines the efficacy of punishment but also can become extremely difficult to enforce. Not surprisingly the problems of running this kind of 'turnstile' system of punishment has brought it into disuse (Morrison, 1985). Limiting penal capacity without effecting any change of 'input' into the penal system is likely to intensify existing problems and may well present some new difficulties.

Clearly 'deep end' strategies of this type are of limited applicability as the primary point of intervention. However, where 'deep end' strategies might be more relevant is in changing the 'intensity' of confinement. That is, there are persuasive arguments for developing different levels of security, including in turn shorter sentences, which could provide gradations in the level of confinement and the adoption of appropriate levels of restraint. As John Conrad has suggested, there are definite advantages in balancing the intensity of confinement with the length of confinement:

> From appropriate restraint it follows that the prison, or the system of prisons, must allow for different security requirements for all those who are imprisoned. Not only does it make no sense to maintain a peaceable cheque writer in maximum security, but it is also a prodigal waste of a scarce and costly resource. No prisoner should be assigned to more security than the safety of the public and the system require.
>
> (Conrad, 1985: 127)

Although in many countries prisoners are classified according to the level of
seriousness of the offence committed, it remains the case that prisoners of all
types are normally kept in unnecessarily restrictive confinement. The
preoccupation with prison security turn penal institutions into fortresses and
means that a large percentage of prisoners are kept under conditions which
bear little relation either to the threat which they pose to public safety or to
the seriousness of the crime which they have committed.

Considerations about the intensity of confinement could be linked to the
length of confinement. For there must come a point when (whatever
measures of effectiveness are employed) diminishing returns set in very
rapidly. For many offenders this point may be reached relatively early in the
sentence when more extensive use of extended home visits, halfway houses,
work release programmes and intermittent custody might be more
appropriate (McConville and Hall Williams, 1985). In short there is a need
to employ different mixes of restriction and mobility combined with different
levels of supervision (Quinn, 1984).

The recent proposal for the introduction of intermittent sentences in
England and Wales which might have facilitated a movement in the right
direction was resisted by some penal reformers and eventually by the
government on the basis that it might be more widely used as an alternative
to existing alternatives rather than decreasing the reliance on custody
(Hudson, 1985; Home Office, 1984). This is a lame and evasive response.
The problem is to ensure that reforms are used for the purpose for which they
were designed. There are no guarantees with reforms but the rejection of
proposals on the basis that they might not work as intended is grossly
inadequate.

Thus 'deep end' strategies which effect greater gradations and refinements
in the system and which serve to make prisons less like warehouses and
fortresses could be useful 'positive' reforms. Like other 'deep end' strategies
they would also need to be supplemented by a series of 'shallow end'
interventions designed to divert from custody large numbers of feckless and
trivial offenders who end up in prison often because of the lack of availability
of more constructive options.

The development of mechanisms to act as alternatives to custody has
gained considerable momentum in the post-war period. A multiplicity of
strategies has been designed to respond to offenders in non-custodial forms
at every point in the criminal justice process. A major concern has been with
attempting to identify the most effective points of intervention in order to
reduce the influx of people to prison. The rationalization of new community-
based sanctions is normally framed within a policy to reduce the overall level
of imprisonment. This reductionist stance is itself linked to a commitment to
minimalism which is concerned with reducing the level of state interference,
coercion and influence. Since this is a major organizing principle within the
debate in penal reform, and since there are important points of similarity and
difference between minimalism and realism, it is necessary to examine briefly

the nature of minimalism before going on to examine some of the issues involved in pursuing 'shallow end' initiatives.

Minimalism

Minimalism, or minimal statism as it is sometimes called, comes in a variety of forms. It has been associated with the 'small is beautiful' movement, radical non-interventionism and a range of anti-bureaucratic movements (S. Cohen, 1983; Schur, 1973; Christie, 1978). It draws on a wide range of political support and includes disillusioned liberals, fiscal conservatives, sentimental anarchists, and libertarian socialists. Fuelled by visions of *1984*, 'net-widening' and the spread of the 'carceral', minimalists are suspicious of state interventionism and tend to favour policies aimed at decentralization, diversion, decarceration and decriminalization.

The minimalist critique of bureaucratic state institutions takes a number of forms but in the main it sees state intervention as too intrusive and as limiting personal freedom. Being too intrusive, it is argued, leads to an overloading of system capacity and ultimately to general ineffectiveness (Scheerer, 1986).

In the penal sphere minimalists argue for the removal of overcrowding as the primary objective, and of the removal of as many offenders as possible from institutions as the general aim. In its more extreme versions minimalists argue that offenders should be kept out of prisons at any price. The brutalizing and negative effects of institutionalization are such that the more people who can be removed or diverted from penal institutions the better. The long-term goal is to reduce the prison population to an 'essential' core.

Clearly there are few people who are not interested in doing something about overcrowding, and there are a range of offenders – mentally ill people, some drug addicts, fine defaulters, and so on – about whom there is some discernible consensus that they ought to be removed from prison (Parliamentary All-Party Penal Affairs Group 1980). But, when other categories of offenders are included, this theoretical and political consensus begins to fracture, as does the general suggestion that reducing the size of the prison population is the solution in itself.

But the endless critiques of the prison – the perennial claims that prisons have 'failed' and the often-repeated assertion that anything is preferable to incarceration – have obscured some of the problems of pursuing a strict minimalist policy. In the desperate rush to deinstitutionalize populations in the past a number of processes have occurred which were not anticipated. These include:

1 *Transcarceration*: The removal of people from formal penal institutions does not preclude the possibility that they will be diverted into other segregative institutions which operate with more benign labels. They may,

for example, be shifted to 'facilities' in the private or medical sector or other forms of confinement. Thus, for example, many 'decarcerated' mental patients have been redirected towards prisons or private custodial institutions (Scull, 1987).

2 *Displacement*: The focus on the reduction of the penal sphere may allow or indeed foster the development of other agencies which may be no more desirable or effective than the existing ones. Moreover, the urgency to remove people from prison may have other effects. As N. Morris has warned:

We face a difficult trade off. We risk substituting more pervasive but less punitive control mechanisms over a vastly larger number of citizens for our present discriminatory and irrational selection of fewer citizens for more primitive and draconian punishments.

(Morris, 1974: 10)

Without succumbing to functionalism we can acknowledge this as a possibility if no simultaneous re-structuring of the alternatives occurs. However, in a sense we have a bleaker picture emerging at present – the development of more pervasive mechanisms of control and the simultaneous expansion of the prison.

3 *Increased discretion*: The focus upon diversion necessarily involves a shift in the level of discretion away from the judicial sphere and provides the possibility for constructing a less accountable and less responsive criminal justice system. Much of the emphasis upon diversion has shifted discretion in ways which may be at odds with needs of certain groups of victims (Sanders, 1988). Similarly the use of early release and amnesties not only brings into question the credibility of the courts but also shifts the locus of discretion into more administrative and less accountable realms (Austin, 1986).

4 *Double tracking*: Minimalist policies tend to overlook the fact that, in the attempt to divert particular populations, prison remains at the hub of the system. Thus, although it may be justifiable to attempt to remove imprisonment as a formal sanction for certain offences, it is possible that unless the alternatives are clearly conceived they could instigate indirect routes back to the prison. The salient example of this process was the attempt to make soliciting-type offences non-imprisonable in England and Wales in 1983. The result was that the level of fines increased dramatically and many women who were unable to pay the fines found themselves imprisoned for non-payment. The overall result was that the number of women convicted of soliciting who were incarcerated in 1984 for non-payment of fines rose dramatically (Criminal Law Revision Committee, 1984).

5 *Benign neglect*: Although there is general agreement that incarceration is

a brutalizing and alienating experience it does not mean that leaving offenders alone or simply returning them to 'the community' is an adequate response. Many of those who end up in prison suffer from a range of deprivations and social and personal problems. Ignoring these material constraints and adopting a policy of benign neglect can leave serious problems unaddressed – as became apparent in the attempts to deinstitutionalize status offenders in America (Handler and Zatz, 1982).

Thus strategies aimed primarily at reducing the prison population through diversion, decarceration and other policies may, if not carefully considered and implemented, produce other problems. For in implementing policies designed to reduce the prison population, it is rarely a question of imprisonment versus non-interventionism. It is rather a matter of attempting to develop a more systematic approach towards decarceration; one which not only attempts to address the issue of state coercion but also maximises the level of public accountability (Kinsey *et al.*, 1986).

Where minimalism involves the re-evaluation of existing practices, the improvement of services, the creation of a more effective division of labour and the reduction of costs, it represents a positive movement. Where it is primarily or exclusively concerned with 'rolling back the state' or where it is openly anti-state it parts company with radical realism. For realists a primary task is the restructuring of state agencies in order to make them more responsive, more effective and more accountable. The apparently contradictory aim is to attempt to develop forms of state organization which protect our liberties but do not over-restrict our lives. To see state intervention as a problem *per se*, however, is to overlook the significant role which the state plays in mediating conflicts, reducing interpersonal violence, redistributing resources and mediating the impact of market forces. It also overlooks the fact that freedom of choice in our society is structured by access to property and that poverty itself is a form of unfreedom. A major function of any state activity, which is concerned with maximizing personal freedom, and promoting justice, must necessarily be to moderate the effects of property differentials (G. Cohen, 1981).

In some cases effectiveness and accountability may be increased through non-state form, involving various modes of privatization, but in other situations they may involve the expansion of existing state agencies and institutions (Matthews, 1989). In the field of criminal justice, for example, there are strong arguments for extending state intervention into a number of 'new crimes' (child abuse, racial and sexual harassment, etc.) and for reducing the use of criminal law in other areas (eg. corporate crime) and for dealing with infractions by more administrative means (Braithwaite and Fisse, 1987; Chapters 1, 4 and 5 in this volume). It is a question of remaining sensitive to the shape and texture of crime.

In the field of penal policy the reduction of the prison population may be an immediate and necessary goal. But achieving this objective is not sufficient in itself. Even if the prison population were to be significantly reduced there would still remain the basic problems concerning the organization, the constituency and the form of incarceration. In short, a realist penal policy must consider the quality as well as the quantity of provision.

In response to the general despondency expressed by both minimalists and abolitionists over the role of alternatives, realists call for specificity and differentiation (see K. Harris, 1985). That is, for a detailed empirical examination of which measures work for which populations under which conditions. Simultaneously it is necessary to differentiate between sanctions which operate primarily in place of prison and those which perform other functions. Dismissing the use and development of alternatives to custody seriously restricts the possibilities for movement, and by implication suggests that the preferred alternative to incarceration is non-intervention. In a limited number of cases non-intervention may be appropriate, but to advocate it as a general policy would be politically untenable and socially unacceptable. Consequently a realist approach is necessarily engaged in the search for more adequate alternatives.

The search for alternatives

Many of the 'first generation' of alternatives which were designed to draw offenders away from prison have proved ambiguous in their effects (Bottoms, 1987). As a result there are currently emerging mixed and at times contradictory responses. On the one hand, some reformers are rapidly losing interest in the development of alternatives in general, while on the other hand there are those who have become more desperate in their search for new remedies and novel answers.

The combination of desperation and pessimism has led to pragmatism. In the formulation of a second generation of alternatives in the 1980s there has been a growing preoccupation with surveillance, intensive monitoring, restrictions on personal movements and the extension of supervisory activities. As Kay Harris has pointed out:

> Many of the new programs seem to be based on the view that the objective is to intimidate the offender and that surveillance, surprise visits, searches and threats produce the best motivation. This new generation of alternatives seems to favour using repressive means in trying to secure obedience and control. Many programs reflect a belief that it is not only appropriate, but highly desirable, to exercise ongoing domination and control over offenders' daily lives; they demand strict adherence to behaviours and conditions developed on the basis of prevailing assumptions about how offenders should live.
>
> (K. Harris, 1983: 168)

The search for alternatives continues. Even within the prevailing mood of pragmatism there is still the feeling that if only the right alternative could be found the penal crisis could be overcome. Something which is more flexible and adaptable, more rigorous and yet more sensitive could provide the remedy for our current ills. In consequence every other year a new measure is promoted which in itself is held to provide the solution. The latest of the new alternatives are electronic monitoring and house arrest, which although carrying high aspirations have, as yet, had little real effect (Ball *et al.*, 1988; Berry and Matthews, 1989). After an initial flurry of enthusiasm each alternative seems sooner or later to meet the same fate and falls out of favour. Either it does not address the right population, or it is too vague, too soft, or it is too expensive.

We seem to be caught in a dilemma. It is clear that we need to develop viable alternatives to custody if we are to reduce the penal population and provide more constructive responses to crime. Yet successive alternatives have failed to live up to expectations, while in some cases their implementation appears to have made matters worse. In fact, the realization is slowly dawning that the solution cannot be found in the endless pursuit of alternatives and by simply offering more of the same. The current disillusionment is thus understandable. However, through the development of more realistic alternatives to custody combined with a more effective process of implementation, there are possible ways out of the present impasse.

The debate about alternatives to custody has recently taken a new direction. It has been recognized that many of the existing so-called alternatives were never really designed as competing alternatives to custody. They were implemented to serve other populations and perform different functions (Harland and Harris, 1984). As 'soft' options they are in many cases not seen as appropriate sanctions for serious offenders and they are adopted by the judiciary only under pressure. In consequence, sentencing options have tended to oscillate between extremes. The choice often appears to be between an alienating term of imprisonment or 'letting the offender off' with a fine, suspended sentence or community service (see Chapter 3 in this volume; Currie, 1985; M. Smith, 1984).

There is clearly, therefore, a need to develop competing, middle-range, sanctions if the judiciary are to be encouraged to use non-custodial sentences more often. The development of such options can be achieved in three ways:

1 *Intensification of existing 'soft' options*: This is to some extent already happening in relation to probation, both in the USA and Britain (Petersilia, 1988). However, there is a danger that it only intensifies sanctions directed towards populations which are already adequately dealt with in less punitive ways. Where this is seen to occur the intensification of existing options may be actively resisted by the relevant agencies (K. Harris, 1985).

2 *Packaging of sanctions*: Existing sanctions are used in combination to offer a formidable but diverse range of sanctions which can be tailored to the requirements of each individual offender. The problem which can arise with packaging is that it becomes very difficult to monitor and evaluate the effectiveness of any particular option.

3 *Innovation*: New sanctions are developed which could be justified in terms of filling the gaps in the range of existing dispositions or which might act as an appropriate sanction for particular types of offender. Electronic monitoring and new forms of surveillance could be given as examples of this option. However, precautions must be taken to ensure that the new options do not duplicate or merely supplement existing sanctions.

If these alternatives are to be effective and have a significant impact upon the existing level of incarceration they must aim to divert a very large percentage of the penal population – particularly the middle- and long-term offenders away from prison. For as Bottomley and Pease have estimated, if we were to 'attempt to reduce the sentenced prison population by a mere 17%, over half the custodial decisions of the courts would have to be substituted by non-custodial decisions' (Bottomley and Pease, 1986: 107).

But even if more 'middle-range' sentencing options were to be introduced there would still remain the difficult problem of implementation and, more precisely, the exact point of implementation – either in relation to the offender or the criminal justice system. Different 'alternatives' are likely to have different effects at different points in the 'criminal career' of the offender, and therefore alternative options need to be considered in terms of their specific point of intervention. It is becoming clear that if 'alternatives' are not to be (mis)used then the framework in which sentencing decisions are made needs to be restructured.

Sentencing policy

Increasingly the sentencing process has become identified as the pivotal point in the criminal justice system. Renewed emphasis on sentencing has been fostered by two related developments. The first is the growing body of research which indicates that the courts are becoming more punitive. In England and Wales the percentage of offenders given immediate custodial sentences has risen from 13.1 per cent in 1980 to 18 per cent in 1987, despite the fact that imprisonment is formally supposed to be used only when all other options have been exhausted (Home Office, 1988b). The second is the knowledge that a decrease of as little as 10 per cent in the length of prison sentences handed out in England and Wales would be enough to remove the problem of overcrowding (Fitzmaurice and Pease, 1982).

In response to these two considerations the problem of implementing a successful decarceration policy appears to lie with limiting judicial discretion by providing rational guidelines. The unsystematic and often idiosyncratic nature of decision-making in the courts as well as the different sentencing patterns between sexes, races and classes have heightened the demands for sentencing reform (see Chapters 1, 5 and 6 in this volume). Without a coherent sentencing policy it is virtually impossible to organize a rational penal policy (Ashworth, 1983).

It was the combination of these concerns which gave the impetus to the attempts to try to implement more determinate forms of sentencing policy in the 1970s and early 1980s. Adopting a more legalistic and 'just deserts' approach, the aim was to set limits on maximum sentences and to apply only the least restrictive penalty in each case. This could, it was claimed, reduce the level of incarceration and also help to reduce the level of crime. Implementation of the 'just deserts' approach, however, did not achieve either objective. Instead, the prison population grew even faster and the rate of recorded crime continued to increase.

There were a number of reasons why determinate sentencing policy did not achieve its objectives. The first was that reformers overlooked, or underestimated, the high degree of informalism which is involved in the sentencing process. Only a small percentage of cases go the full distance and many are settled 'out of court' or in the 'shadow of the law' (Mnookin and Kornhauser, 1979). The prevalence of plea-bargaining and various 'negotiated' settlements meant that any reform policy which focused exclusively on the formal processes was likely to be of limited relevance. The second major problem which confronted determinate sentencing policies was that many of the decisions affecting outcomes occur outside the court and involve a number of agencies who are not directly responsible for passing sentence (Bottomley, 1973). The third obstacle to the effective implementation of determinate sentencing policy was the essentially individualized nature of justice. This means that because of the differences between individuals and the specificity of each case, the quest for uniform sentencing outcomes may be an inappropriate aim. Also, the rejection of 'treatment' and 'welfare' considerations resulted in less emphasis being placed upon contextual personal circumstances as mitigating factors (Walker, 1976). In this way individual disparities were not only maintained but also often accentuated. Finally, by providing guidelines for a range of maximum sentence lengths determinate sentencing actually increased the level of judicial discretion and encouraged the implementation of generally longer sentences (Greenberg and Humphries, 1980; Davies, 1985).

The disillusionment which arose from the attempt to implement determinate sentencing policies led to the recommendation that there should be a more thoroughgoing and co-ordinated approach to sentencing in the form of sentencing councils or commissions. Much recent attention has been focused upon Minnesota where a sentencing commission has attempted to reduce sentencing disparities and match sentencing decisions to the available level of prison capacity. By linking public policy to the public purse it has not only questioned the cost of punishment but also asked how much punishment can we afford.

The first year of the policy appeared to be reasonably successful and Minnesota is achieving its goal of keeping down the level of incarceration (C. Moore and Meithe, 1986; Mullen, 1987). However, there are signs that this approach, like determinate sentencing reforms, is unlikely to provide the desired results. There is already evidence that prosecutors are developing new bargaining practices and reverting to their previous sentencing policies. Also although the prison population kept within the guidelines for the first year (1981) it has increased substantially in subsequent years. Additionally there is a sense in which the problem of discretion has not been so much resolved as displaced. That is, it has shifted from the judicial arena into an even less accountable administrative network. The administrative organization of 'justice' appears distant, impersonal and where it remains tied to the 'justice model', as it does in Minnesota, it appears inflexible and insensitive. As a result

> The principal criticisms of the guidelines in operation were that they were too rigid, that they shifted too much power to the prosecutor, and that failure to set standards for non-prison sentences exacerbated pre-existing disparities in imposition of jail sentences.
>
> (Tonry, 1987: 29)

Minnesota has been (prematurely?) hailed as a 'success' and as a model for other sentencing bodies. In comparison to the other sentencing commissions which have been set up in Maine, Connecticut, South Carolina and New York, which were all generally unsuccessful, it does seem to have achieved some limited objectives, although these may be only temporary. The long-term effectiveness of a sentencing commission does not look very promising and, as with a number of other sentencing reforms, they are deceptively difficult to implement and enforce. This is partly because of the peculiarly complex nature of the sentencing process itself and the difficulties of overcoming the resistance which judges and prosecutors exhibit in the face of new policies being imposed upon them. The judiciary, we are continually reminded, are a powerful and resilient body and the implication is that any radical reform of the sentencing process which does not have their co-operation will be extremely difficult to implement and sustain.

This means that any form of 'top down' or imposed policy is likely to have little success and that there is a need to rethink the process of decision-making in such a way that the judiciary are involved in the proposed changes and are generally complicit in the reform process itself. One possible way in which this might be achieved is through the development of an inter-agency approach to sentencing.

Inter-agency co-operation

Realist criminologists have been at the forefront of those who have promoted inter-agency co-operation as an important means for effecting reform within the criminal justice system (Kinsey *et al.*, 1986; Matthews, 1986). Particularly in the areas of policing, crime prevention and juvenile justice, inter-agency approaches have been successful where other strategies have failed. This is primarily because of the interrelated network of agencies which operate within the criminal justice system. As a result any thorough-going reform will invariably involve the co-operation of a number of agencies, while the active resistance of any one agency can block or undermine even the most well-thought-out policy. As each option usually has a particular range of applicability it also requires an agreed framework for effective implementation.

> Both the need for and the difficulty of creating a distinct entity for dialogue and action concerning the implementation of alternatives to incarceration stem from the very broad array of actors who play a role in the way the criminal justice system operates. In other words, the interdependence of the system's different components and the ability of actors in one part to nullify or redirect changes made in another virtually guarantee that successful alternatives must be a group process.
>
> (Harland and Harris, 1987: 85)

The experience in England and Wales reinforces the point. All too often well-intentioned reforms have failed to take the principal agencies along and have floundered. However, where inter-agency approaches have been implemented around particular objectives the results have been impressive. In the field of juvenile diversion, for instance, inter-agency initiatives have proved extremely effective. In Northamptonshire, Basingstoke and elsewhere, inter-agency co-operation has been established in order to achieve a reduction in the use of custody for juveniles through the creation of what have been termed 'non-custodial zones' (Gibson, 1986). Levels of juvenile incarceration have been significantly reduced. Most importantly the resistance of the judiciary has been overcome and new levels of dialogue and co-ordination have been achieved. Employing the existing range of alternatives, and in one case placing more emphasis upon the use of police cautioning this approach has largely avoided the 'net-widening' problem and has diverted a considerable number of juveniles away from the mainstream of the system. Harris and Webb conclude:

> These instances entail not only a multi-level systemic approach to a local juvenile justice system but also the propitious circumstances of broad system consensus with the aim of the programme itself,

including (at worst) passive acquiescence from the police, the experts, court officials and administrators, sentencers and key community figures. Where this support is not present, or is withdrawn, either the programme fails through the lack of use, or it sustains itself through the absorption of the kind of marginal delinquent whom it had previously been anxious to exclude.

(R. Harris and Webb, 1987: 165)

The implications are that it is important to build consensus around the aims of intervention, that each of the relevant agencies involved in implementing the policy must be directly involved and that diversion policies of this kind are likely to be most effective with 'low risk' groups.

Inter-agency approaches of this type also have the additional advantage of providing new forms of accountability by opening up discussion about the nature of dispositions. Moreover, they can be organized around local circumstances and thereby remain responsive to varying perceptions of the problem of crime in different localities.

No matter how well formulated particular proposals might be or how 'realistic' they seem, without a proper framework for intervention there is little likelihood that they will meet expectations. Developing competing alternatives is no doubt a necessary step and allows for greater flexibility, but without co-operation and discussion between the agencies involved the results will invariably be uncertain.

There will inevitably be difficulties in setting up inter-agency co-operation and there will almost certainly be rivalries between the various professional groupings. There will also be the problem of determining the relationship between agencies and of deciding on priorities and formulating objectives. However, it now seems abundantly clear that the development of an effective policy of decarceration must be predicated upon the establishment of some kind of inter-agency alliance able to organize the appropriate use of alternatives in specific contexts and in relation to designated populations. The challenge which confronts us is to draw upon those examples of inter-agency co-operation which have proved successful in the field of juvenile corrections and adapt them to the mainstream of the adult system.

A critical factor in the process, which is often overlooked by criminologists, is the attitude of the general public. The experience of countries like the Netherlands suggests that the level of public tolerance plays a crucial part in conditioning the overall use and level of incarceration (Downes, 1988).

What the public wants

So far I have tried to fit together some of the parts of the puzzle. In doing so I have focused mainly on the formal agencies and processes which need to be considered when thinking about penal reform. However there is a growing recognition amongst realist criminologists and others that there is a need to take public opinion seriously. This is not only because the level of public tolerance is a critical variable in creating 'crime' but also because of the significant relation between formal and informal interests in determining the nature of sanctions (Lea, 1987).

The criminologist has for some time offered a contradictory picture of the public interest in crime and punishment. Either the public have been presented as being totally preoccupied with the problem of crime and as extremely punitive; or they are presented as being ignorant of the real incidence of crime and as basically indifferent to the issue of punishment. Both these conceptions on closer examination turn out to be deficient (Wright, 1988). This however does not divest these twin ideologies of their political utility. For on the one hand they present policy-makers as moderate arbitrators; while on the other hand they obscure the issue of accountability, since administrators cannot be expected to answer to a public which is wilfully ignorant or indifferent.

Although there is some support for segregative responses to certain crimes the growing body of research from a number of countries indicates that the public are more reasonable and sophisticated than we have been led to believe (Walker and Hough, 1988). The public it would seem want protection, value for money and a range of sanctions which express disapproval but not necessarily in the form of incarceration.

In the first British Crime Survey, for example, victims were asked about what 'their' offenders deserved. Only 50 per cent even wanted the offender brought to court, only 10 per cent wanted a custodial sentence, while approximately 30 per cent wanted some form of reparation or compensation. These findings were generally reinforced by the findings from the second *British Crime Survey*, which found a high degree of 'leniency' among victims and a preference for compensation and community-service for non-violent offenders (Hough and Mayhew, 1983; Hough and Moxon, 1985). Similar findings have been recorded in the USA. In one survey of 600 interviews conducted in Maryland which set out to compare the priorities of policy-makers and the general public examining in particular their respective views on the aims of punishments, it was found that:

> While the policy makers feel that the public prefers (in this case by a wide margin) the goal of incapacitation, this goal is in fact the second lowest priority in the public view. While policy makers likewise feel that the general public strongly supports the goal of retributive punishment (also in this case, by a wide margin on the original metric) this goal is actually assigned the lowest priority by our sample of the public. It is therefore not surprising that while the policy makers feel that the goal of rehabilitation would be the lowest in the public esteem (and by a very wide margin indeed) this goal is in fact tied with that of deterrence for the public's highest priority.
>
> (Gottfredson and Taylor, 1987: 62)

The prioritization of rehabilitation and general deterrence amongst the general public is not difficult to understand. For they as the actual and potential victims of crime have a vested interest in ensuring that offenders are not further marginalized and debilitated as a result of punishment but that they receive a sanction which expresses public disapproval of their action and which will simultaneously make them less of a social liability. Not surprisingly there seems to be a broad consensus that only the most serious and violent offenders should be imprisoned. Even in these cases the public would appear to welcome less damaging and more constructive forms of incarceration.

In dismissing the rehabilitative ideal in the 1970s criminologists did the general public a great disservice. The 'burial' of the rehabilitative ideal did however allow the further reduction of resources in the prison. Although it was the case that the notion of rehabilitation had been narrowly conceived as a purely psychological readjustment rather than as a social process involving re-establishing the links between the offender and the wider community, the willingness with which many criminologists embraced the 'death' of the rehabilitative ideal indicates how out of touch they were with the interests and concerns of the general public.

Whereas the critics of rehabilitation argued that its realization undermined the efficacy of punishment it would appear in retrospect that it was the obsession with punishment which eroded the prospects of developing a viable rehabilitative policy. Rather than dismiss the rehabilitative ideal a criminology which was responsive to public concerns would have attempted to find ways to turn the ideal into a reality.

But taking notice of public attitudes is important for other reasons. The changes in the levels of public tolerance can have a profound influence on the climate in which penal reform is organized. Although there may be significant differences between public and official responses public tolerance places parameters on the possibilities of reform and can be a critical factor in developing effective decarceration policies. It is therefore necessary for any radical reform strategy to engage directly with public opinion. This task should not only aim to gather and reproduce public opinion but also use public opinion surveys as a basis for formulating policies. There are four dimensions which could be usefully developed: educative, interconnecting, engaging and enabling.

1 *Educative*: The first level of engagement provides basic information for policy-makers and sentencers about the prioritization of public concerns about crime, and attitudes towards sentencing policies.
2 *Interconnecting*: The second level involves the possibility of providing links and sharing knowledge between disparate groups and factions who otherwise might remain unaware of how their interests and concerns relate to other groups.
3 *Engaging*: The dissemination and publication of information about public

attitudes to crime and punishment could provide the basis of a wider public discourse on these issues. In particular it might facilitate debate about the purposes and effects of punishment.

4 *Enabling*: The information gathered and the ensuing public debate could provide a basis for mobilization of campaigns and pressure groups which in turn might extend the parameters of reform.

It is becoming evident that an effective decarceration strategy would benefit from increases in the level of public tolerance and the expression of public support for alternatives. It would be preferable if this also involved greater public participation in decision-making processes. It is, however, not just a matter of trying to persuade the general public to be more tolerant. The public – however badly misrepresented – cannot be expected to give up existing safeguards, ineffective as they may be, without the provision of more constructive measures. If penal reformers are to reduce the number of people in prison, they will have to engage with the public and persuade them of their case. *They may also have to be prepared to listen.*

Effective punishments

It has been suggested that there is a need to develop competing alternatives to prison which allow a greater range of sentencing options. It has also been suggested that these are likely to be effective only if they are implemented in a co-ordinated and systematic way. Further it has been argued that if the general public are to endorse these new sanctions they must adequately reflect public interests and carry rehabilitative potential. They should also ideally have an educational value, allow for the expression of remorse, and ultimately help to re-establish relations between the offender and the community. This is why in principle sanctions such as community service represent positive innovations. Reparation schemes and compensation orders also meet some of the criteria and their use could be extended (D. Smith *et al.*, 1988).

But what about imprisonment itself? It has already been suggested that consideration ought to be given to rethinking the 'intensity' of confinement, rather than treating all inmates as if they were mass murderers or psychopaths. The implication is that such a policy woud serve to decrease the level of segregation and thereby open up the relationship between 'exclusive' and 'inclusive' modes of regulation. Pessimistic critics are likely to depict such movements as the 'dispersal of discipline' and the spreading of the prison into the community (Bottoms, 1983; Christie, 1978; S. Cohen, 1977). These critics, however, tend to overlook the possibility that such a movement would simultaneously involve the opening up of the prison to the community. The more open the relationship between the prison and the wider community the greater the possibilities for the development of state-obligated rehabilitation programmes, work release, retraining and the broadening of educational provision. Clearly within prison the minimum aim must be to avoid the debilitation of offenders and where possible to develop competences (Morris, 1974). Many community-based facilities typically offer a range of programmes for minor offenders some of which are innovative and imaginative. Some of these could usefully be incorporated within the framework of the prison.

Reducing the intensity of segregation might also facilitate greater levels of accountability. Public representatives could play a much greater part in organizing and monitoring the prison system and could publish regular reports. Allied to the issue of accountability is the problem of determining the effectiveness of different institutions. For too long criminologists and policy-makers have relied upon the inadequate and often misleading measure of recidivism (Wilson, 1980). It is time that this yardstick was replaced.

> Instead, the effectiveness of an official performance should be taped by evaluating his or her ability to establish viable programmes that facilitate the acquisition and interpersonal and occupational skills by inmates. For instance each institution should be monitored and compared on such measures as the percentage of inmates participating in treatment programmes, the average number of hours that an inmate spends in rehabilitation programmes, what is done during this time ('programme integrity'); the number of education degrees carried, the number of former inmates placed in jobs related to the training they received in prison, and the size of work release populations.
>
> (Cullen and Gilbert, 1982: 269)

There may be differences of opinion over the establishment of the most appropriate sets of criteria against which the effectiveness of incarceration is to be assessed, but meaningful criteria need to be developed. As with schools and hospitals, the criteria of effectiveness for the penal system cannot be reduced to the listing of its 'failures'. Imagine, for example, if schools were assessed primarily by the number of people who failed examinations or hospitals on the number of patients who died. Prisons should be assessed in terms of their achievements, the provision programmes and the level and quality of services which they deliver.

One effect of the recent movement towards private prisons has been to raise the question of how prisons might be effectively monitored (Taylor and Pease, 1989; Gentry, 1986). The privatization debate has also explicitly raised the issue of how imprisonment can be reorganized and improved. Both critics and supporters have argued that it would not be difficult to design anything which was much worse than the existing penal institutions (Shaw, 1987b; Adam Smith Institute, 1984). This debate stands in contrast to the 'radical' critique of the prison which claims that prisons are beyond reform and have 'failed' ever since their inception. These negative responses, like the dismissal of rehabilitation, have provided a useful justification for leaving prisons essentially unchanged rather than encouraging the exploration of more progressive options.

Conclusion

Positive penal reforms are both necessary and overdue. Reformers can no longer claim that they lack public or political support. Moreover, there *could* be votes in prisons – if constructive policies were to be pursued. It is becoming widely recognized not only that there are very few votes in building more and more prisons but also that the current prison-building programme is not going to resolve the problem, (Lea *et al.*, 1986; Stern, 1987) despite the enormous amount of taxpayers' money involved. On the contrary, the building of new institutions and the provision of more places may encourage the greater use of incarceration in the future. Thus even with a £1 billion prison-building programme there will still be 20,000 cells without integral sanitation in England and Wales by the end of the century.

The prison-building programme at best offers the possibility of short-term relief of overcrowding while awaiting the implementation of an effective decarceration policy. At worst it serves as a way of not facing up to, or of postponing, the problem of penal reform. It is in essence a policy which is both expensive and evasive. It is the preferred option for those who do not really want to grasp the nettle of penal reform.

Yet calls for the wholesale abolition of prisons are unrealistic, as abolitionists themselves have come to realize. The resolution of the penal crisis does not reside in simply removing people from prisons at all costs. Reducing prison size through sentencing policies or commissions or by administrative techniques has proved difficult to realize; neither will the solution to the penal problem be found in the adoption of any *one* particular sanction. What it is important to know is exactly *how* any particular sanction fits into the sentencing structure and in which type of cases it is to be used. Such sanctions need to be justified positively in terms of their appropriateness and their social utility rather than purely negatively as the 'other' of incarceration. In the immediate future the most challenging penal problem in many advanced industrial countries will be to remove the problem of prison overcrowding (Heinz, 1988; Faugeron, 1988). This will be necessary not only in order to avoid the detrimental and dangerous effects that overcrowding has on both prisoners and the prison regime, but also for more general political and practical reasons. The preoccupation with overcrowding serves to deflect attention away from the more endemic problems facing the prison and it encourages the adoption of narrow managerialist stances which view the overall problem in terms of 'inputs' and 'outputs'. By creating a permanent 'state of emergency' it encourages the proliferation of stopgap measures rather than long-term solutions. Resolving the problem of overcrowding and instigating legally enforceable minimum conditions of containment is therefore a priority.

But the removal of overcrowding does not require or justify 'exceptional' measures. Rather, as with the general objective of reconstructing the prison population it requires a combined offensive involving at least four processes: first, the development of more realistic and appropriate sanctions which can act as competing alternatives to prison; second, the implementation of these sanctions in a co-ordinated way in order that they are applied at the most effective point in the process; third, the setting of priorities and the formulation of targets through direct engagement with public opinion; and fourth, the encouragement of public support for realistic alternatives and the creation of a 'culture of tolerance'. Achieving these objectives would be facilitated by the deconstruction of the existing penal fortresses and the setting-up of more open and accountable institutions. These, with their differential levels of security, might encourage not so much the spread of the prison into the community but rather the expansion of the community into the prison.

Bibliography

Adam Smith Institute (1984) *Omega Report* London, Justice Policy.
Advisory Council on the Penal System (1970) *Non-Custodial and Semi-Custodial Penalties*, London, HMSO.
Allen, H. (1987) *Justice Unbalanced: Gender, Psychiatry and Judicial Decisions*, Milton Keynes, Open University Press.
——— (1988) 'One law for all reasonable persons?', *International Journal of the Sociology of Law*, 16, 419–32.
Ashworth, A. (1983) *Sentencing and Penal Policy*, London, Weidenfeld and Nicolson.
Ashworth, A., Genders, E., Mansfield, G., Peay, J. and Player, E. (1984) *Sentencing in the Crown Court: Report of an Exploratory Study*, Occasional Paper no. 10, Oxford, Centre for Criminological Research.
Austin, J. (1986) 'Using early release to relieve prison crowding: a dilemma of public policy', *Crime and Delinquency* 32, 4: 404–503.
Austin, J. and Krisberg, B. (1982) 'The unmet promises of alternatives to incarceration', *Crime and Delinquency* 28: 374–409.
Bakal, Y. and Polsky, H. (1978) *Reforming Correctional Institutions for Juvenile Offenders*, Lexington, Mass., D.C. Heath.
Ball, R., Huff, C. and Lilly, R. (1988) *House Arrest and Correctional Policy*, London, Sage.
Beccaria, C. (1963) *On Crimes and Punishment*, Indianapolis, Ind., Bobbs-Merrill.
Beltram, G. (1984) *Testing the Safety Net*, London, Bedford Square Press and National Council for Voluntary Organizations.
Benson, M. and Walker, E. (1988) 'Sentencing the white-collar offender', *American Sociological Review* 53: 294–302.
Berry, B. and Matthews, R. (1989) 'Making the right connections: electronic monitoring and house arrest', in R. Matthews (ed.) *Privatising Criminal Justice*, London, Sage.
Blomberg, T. (1987) 'Criminal justice reform and social control: are we becoming a

minimum security society?', in J. Lowman, R. J. Menzies and T. S. Palys *Transcarceration: Essays in the Sociology of Social Control*, Aldershot, Gower.

Blom-Cooper, L. (1988) *The Penalty of Imprisonment*, London, Prison Reform Trust.

Blumstein, A. (1987) 'Sentencing and the prison crowding problem', in S. Gottfredson and S. McConville (eds) *America's Correctional Crisis*, Westport, Conn., Greenwood Press.

Board of Inland Revenue (1988) *130th Annual Report*, Cm 529, London, HMSO.

Borna, S. (1986) 'Free enterprise goes to prison', *British Journal of Criminology* 26, 4, October: 321-34.

Bottomley, K. (1973) *Decisions in the Penal Process*, Oxford, Martin Robertson.

Bottomley, K. and Pease, K. (1986) *Crime and Punishment, Interpreting the Data*, Milton Keynes, Open University Press.

Bottoms, A.E. (1983) 'Neglected features of contemporary penal systems' in D. Garland and P. Young (eds) (1983) *The Power to Punish*, London, Heinemann.

____ (1987) 'Limiting prison size: the experience of England and Wales', *Howard Journal* 26, 3: 177-202.

Box, S. (1987) *Recession, Crime and Punishment*, London, Tavistock.

Box, S. and Hale, C. (1985) 'Unemployment, imprisonment and prison overcrowding', *Contemporary Crises* 9: 208-28.

Boyson, R. (1971) *Down With the Poor*, London, Churchill Press.

____ (1978) *Centre Foreward: A Radical Conservative Programme, London, Maurice Temple Smith.*

Braithwaite, J. and Fisse, B. (1987) 'Self-regulation and the control of corporate crime', in C. Shearing and P. Stenning (eds) *Private Policing*, London, Sage.

Breed, B. (1979) *White-Collar Bird*, London, John Clare. C. Ronalds and M. Richardson.

Brown, D. (1987) 'Politics of reform', in G. Zdenkowski, (eds) *The Criminal Injustice System, Vol. 2*, Australia, Pluto Press.

Burton, J. (1985) *Why No Cuts?*, Hobart Paper no. 24, London, Institute of Economic Affairs.

Byrne, D. (1987) 'Rich and poor: the growing divide', in A. Walker and C. Walker (eds) *The Growing Divide: A Social Audit 1979-1987*, London, Child Poverty Action Group.

Carlen, P. (1976) *Magistrates' Justice*, Oxford, Martin Robertson.

____ (1983a) 'On rights and powers: some notes on penal politics', in D. Garland, and P. Young (eds), *The Power to Punish*, London, Heinemann.

____ (1983b) *Women's Imprisonment: A Study in Social Control*. London, Routledge and Kegan Paul.

____ (1988) *Women, Crime and Poverty*, Milton Keynes, Open University Press.

____ (1989) *Women's Imprisonment: A Strategy for Abolition*, Occasional Paper no. 3, University of Keele Centre for Criminology.

Carlen, P. (ed.) (1985) *Criminal Women*, Cambridge, Polity Press.

Casale, S. and Hillsman, S. (1986) *The Enforcement of Fines as Criminal Sanctions: The English Experience and its Relevance to American Practice*, New York, Vera Institute of Justice.

Chesney-Lind, M. (1978) 'Chivalry re-examined: women and the criminal justice system', in L. Bowker (ed.) (1978) *Women, Crime and the Criminal Justice System*, Lexington, Mass., D.C. Heath.

Christie, N. (1978) 'Prisons in society: or society as a prison: a conceptual analysis', in J. Freeman (ed.) *Prisons Past and Future*, London, Heinemann.

Cohen, G. (1981) 'Freedom, justice and capitalism', *New Left Review* 126, March/April: 3-16.

Cohen, S. (1977) 'Prisons and the future of control systems: from concentration to dispersal', in M. Fitzgerald *et al.* (eds) *Welfare in Action*, London, Routledge & Kegan Paul.

___ (1983) 'Social control talk: telling stories about correctional change', in D. Garland and P. Young (eds) *The Power to Punish*, London, Heinemann.

___ (1985) *Visions of Social Control*, Cambridge, Polity Press.

Conrad, J. (1985) 'Charting a course for imprisonment policy', in *Our Crowded Prisons: The Annals of The American Academy of Political and Social Science*, March: 123-35.

Cook, D. (1988) 'Rich, law, poor law: differential, response to, tax and supplementary, benefit, fraud', unpublished PhD thesis, University of Keele.

___ (1989) *Rich Law, Poor Law: Differential Responses to Tax and Supplementary Benefit Fraud*, Milton Keynes, Open University Press.

CPAG (1988) *National Welfare Benefits Handbook: 18th Edition, 1988/9*, London, Child Poverty Action Group.

CPSA (1984) *Policing the Welfare – Benefits Under Attack*, report of a Special Conference held at University College of Wales, Cardiff, 8 October.

Criminal Injuries Compensation Board (1988) *Twenty-Fourth Report; Accounts for the Year Ended 31 March 1988*, Cm 536, London, HMSO.

Criminal Law Revision Committee (1984) *Sixteenth Report, Prostitution in the Street*, Cmnd 9329, London, HMSO.

Croall, H. (1988) 'Mistakes, accidents, and someone else's fault: the trading offender in court', *Journal of Law and Society* 15, 3: 293-315.

Crow, I. and Simon, F. (1987) *Unemployment and Magistrates' Courts*, London, NACRO.

Cullen, F. and Gilbert, K. (1982) *Reaffirming Rehabilitation*, Cincinatti, Ohio, Anderson Publishing.

Currie, E. (1985) *Confronting Crime: An American Challenge*, New York, Pantheon.

Davies, M. (1985) 'Determinate sentencing reform in California and its impact upon the penal system', *British Journal of Criminology* 25, 1: 1-30.

De Haan, W. (1986) 'Abolitionism and the politics of bad conscience', in H. Bianchi and R. Van Swaaningen (eds) *Abolitionism: Towards a Non-Repressive Approach to Crime*, Amsterdam, Free University Press.

Dine, J. (1988) 'The disqualification of company directors', *The Company Lawyer*, 9, 10: 213-18.

Ditton, J. (1977) *Part-Time Crime*, London, Macmillan.

Downes, D. (1980) 'Abolition: Possibilities and Pitfalls', in A. Bottom and R. Preston (eds) *The Coming Penal Crisis*, Edinburgh, Scottish Academic Press.

___ (1988) *Contrasts in Tolerance: Post War Penal Policy in the Netherlands and England and Wales*, Oxford, Clarendon Press.

Durkheim, E. (1984) *The Division of Labour*, London, Macmillan.

Eaton, M. (1983) 'Mitigating circumstances: the familiar rhetoric', *International Journal of the Sociology of Law* 11: 385ff.

Ericson, R., McMahon, M., and Evans, D. (1987) 'Punishing for profit: reflections on the revival of privatisation in corrections', *Canadian Journal of Criminology* 4, October.

Expenditure Committee (1978) Fifteenth Report, *The Reduction of Pressure on the Penal System*, HC Paper 662, London, HMSO.

Fattah, E. (1987) 'Ideological biases in the evaluation of criminal justice reform', in R. Ratner and J. McMullen (eds) *State Control: Criminal Justice Politics in Canada*, Canada, University of British Columbia Press.

Faugeron, C. (1988) *Prisons in France: An Irresistible Increasing of the Detained Population?*, paper presented to the European Colloquium on Research on Crime and Criminal Justice Policy in Europe, Oxford, July 1988.

Faugeron, C. and Houchon, G. (1987) 'Prisons and the penal system: from penology to the sociology of penal policies', *International Journal of the Sociology of Law* 15: 393–425.

Fisher Committee (1973) *Report of the Committee on Abuse of Social Security Benefits*, Cmnd 5228, London, HMSO.

Fitzmaurice, C. and Pease, K. (1982) 'Prison sentences and population: a comparison of some European countries', *Justice of the Peace* 146: 575–9.

_____ (1986) *The Psychology of Judicial Sentencing*, Manchester, Manchester University Press.

Fraser, D. (1973) *The Evolution of the British Welfare State*, London, Macmillan.

Galanter, M. (1986) 'Legality and its discontents', in H. Blankenburg, E. Jansa and H. Cuthner (eds). *Alternative Rechtsformen und Alternatives Zum Resht*, Westdentcher, Verlag.

Gentry, J. (1986) 'The panoptican re-visited: the problem of monitoring private persons', *Yale Law Journal* 96, 2: 353–75.

Gibson, B. (1986) 'The abolition of custody for juvenile offenders', *Justice of the Peace* 22 November: 739–42.

Golding, P. and Middleton, S. (1982) *Images of Welfare*, Oxford, Martin Robertson.

Gottfredson, S. and Taylor, R. (1987) 'Attitudes of correctional policy – Makers and the public', in S. Gottfredson and S. McConville (eds) *America's Correctional Crisis*, Westport, Conn., Greenwood Press.

Grebing, G. (n.d.) *The Fine in Comparative Law* (English translation of *Die Geldstrafe in deutschen and ausländischen Recht*, Part II, 'Die Geldstrafe in rechtsvergleichander Dartstellung', edited by Hans-Heinrich Jescheck and Gerhart Grebing, Nomos Verlagsgesellschaft, Baden-Baden (1978), trans. Brian Duffett, Cambridge, Institute of Criminology.

Greenberg, D. (1983) 'Reflections in the Justice Model', *Contemporary Crisis* 7: 313–27.

Greenberg, D. and Humphries, D. (1980) 'The co-option of fixed sentencing reform', *Crime and Delinquency* April: 206–25.

Griffith, J. (1977) *The Politics of the Judiciary*, London, Fontana.

Hagan, J. (1988) *Structural Criminology*, Cambridge, Polity Press.

Hagan, J. and Palloni, A. (1986) ' "Club Fed" and the sentencing of white-collar offenders before and after Watergate', *Criminology* 24: 603–22.

Handler, J. and Zatz, J. (1982) *Neither Angels nor Thieves: Studies in the Deinstitutionalisation of Status Offenders*, Washington, DC, National Academy Press.

Harland, A. and Harris, P. (1984) 'Developing and implementing alternatives to incarceration', *University of Illinois Law Review*, 2: 319–64.

_____ (1987) 'Structuring the development of alternatives to incarceration', in S. Gottfredson and S. McConville (eds) *America's Correctional Crisis*, Westport, Conn., Greenwood Press.

Harris, K. (1983) 'Strategies, values and the emerging generation of alternatives to incarceration', *Social Change, XII*, 1983/4: 141–70.

_____ (1985) 'Reducing prison crowding and non-prison penalties', *Annals of the American Academy of Political and Social Science*, 478, March: 150–9.

Harris, R. and Webb, D. (1987) *Welfare, Power and Juvenile Justice*, London, Tavistock.

HC 102 (1983/4) *Committee of Public Accounts: Prevention and Detection Evasion of NI Contributions and of Social Security Benefits*, London, HMSO.

Health and Safety Executive (1988) *Annual Report 1987/8*, London, HMSO.

Heinz, N. (1988) *The Problems of Imprisonment: Including Strategies that Might Be Employed to Minimise the Use of Custody*, paper presented to the European Colloquium on Research on Crime and Criminal Justice Policy in Europe, Oxford, July 1988.

Henry, S. (1983) *Private Justice*, London, Routledge & Kegan Paul.

Home Office (1984) *Intermittent Custody*, Cmnd 9281, London, HMSO.

_____ (1985) *Report of the Parole Board 1984*, London, HMSO.

_____ (1986a) *The Sentence of the Court*, London, HMSO.

_____ (1986b) *The Ethnic Origins of Prisoners: The Prison Population on 30 June 1985 and Persons Received July 1984 to March 1985*, Home Office Statistical Bulletin no 17, June 1986.

_____ (1986c) *Criminal Justice: A Working Paper*, revised ed, London, HMSO.

_____ (1987a) *Report on the Work of the Prison Service 1986-7*, Cmnd 246, London, HMSO.

_____ (1987b) *Probation Statistics, England and Wales 1986*, London, Home Office.

_____ (1987c) *Report of the Parole Board 1986*, London, HMSO.

_____ (1987d) *Criminal Statistics: England and Wales 1986*, London, HMSO.

_____ (1988a) *Punishment, Custody and the Community*, Cm 424, London, HMSO.

_____ (1988b) *Criminal Statistics: England and Wales 1987*, Cm 498, London, HMSO.

_____ (1988c) *Report of the Working Group on the Costs of Crime*, London, Home Office.

_____ (1988d) *Report of the Parole Board 1987*, London, HMSO.

Hough, M. and Mayhew, P. (1983) *The British Crime Survey: First Report*, Home Office Research Study no. 76, London Home Office.

Hough, M. and Moxon, D. (1985) 'Dealing with offenders: popular opinions and views of victims', *Howard Journal* 24, 3: 160–75.

Houghton, Lord (1977) 'Administration, politics and equity', in IEA, *The State of Taxation*, IEA Readings no. 16, London, Institute of Economic Affairs.

Hudson, B. (1985) 'Intermittent custody: a response to the Green Paper', *Howard Journal* 2, 1: 40–51.

_____ (1987) *Justice Through Punishment*, London, Macmillan.

Hulsman, L. (1982) 'Penal reform in the Netherlands: part two', *Howard Journal*, 21, 1:35–47.

_____ (1986) 'Critical criminology and the concept of crime', in H. Bianchi and R. Swaaningen (eds) *Abolitionism: Towards a Non Repressive Approach to Crime*, Amsterdam, Free University Press.

Inland Revenue (1987) *Leaflet 73, How Settlements are Negotiated*, London, HMSO.

Jones, T., Maclean, B. and Young, J. (1986) *The Islington Crime Survey*, Aldershot, Gower.

Keith Committee (1983) *Report on the Enforcement Powers of the Revenue Departments*, Cmnd 8822, London, HMSO.

Kinsey, R., Lea, J. and Young, J. (1986) *Losing the Fight Against Crime*, Oxford, Blackwell.

Klein, M. (1979) 'Deinstitutionalisation and diversion of offenders: a litany of impediments', in N. Morris and M. Tonoy (eds) *Crime and Justice*, Chicago, Ill., University of Chicago Press.

Kornhauser, A. (1978) *Social Sources of Delinquency*, Chicago, Ill., University of Chicago Press.

Kruttschnitt, C. (1982) 'Women, crime and dependency', *Criminology* 19, 4: 495ff, Columbus, Ohio.

Lacey, N. (1988) *State Punishment: Political Principles and Community Values*, London, Routledge.

Lea, J. (1987) 'Left realism: a defence', *Contemporary Crisis*, 11, 371–401.

Lea, J. and Young, J. (1984) *What is to be Done about Law and Order*, Harmondsworth, Penguin.

Lea, J., Matthews, R. and Young, J. (1986) *Law and Order: Five Years On*, Paper no. 2, Middlesex Polytechnic, Centre for Criminology.

Lerman, P. (1984) 'Child welfare, the private sector and community-based corrections', *Crime and Delinquency* 30, 1: 5–38.

Levi, M. (1981) *The Phantom Capitalists: The Organization and Control of Long-Firm Fraud*, Aldershot, Gower.

_____ (1987) *Regulating Fraud: White-Collar Crime and the Criminal Process*, London, Tavistock.

_____ (1989) 'Suite justice: sentencing for fraud', *Criminal Law Review* June: 420–31.

Loney, M. (1986) *The Politics of Greed*, London, Pluto Press.

McConville, S. and Hall Williams, E. (1985) *Crime and Punishment: A Radical Rethink*, Tawney Publications no 32, London.

Mars, G. (1982) *Cheats at Work*, London, Allen & Unwin.

Mathieson, T. (1974) *The Politics of Abolition*, Oxford, Martin Robertson.

_____ (1986) 'The arguments against prison construction', in H. Bianchi and R. Van Swaaningen (eds) *Abolitionism: Towards a Non-Repressive Approach to Crime*, Amsterdam, Free University Press.

Matthews, R. (1986) *Policing Prostitution: A Multi-Agency Approach*, Occasional Paper no. 1, Middlesex Polytechnic, Centre for Criminology.

_____ (1987a) 'Decarceration and social control: fantasies and realities', in J. Lowman, R. J. Menzies and T. S. Palys (eds) *Transcarceration: Essays in the Sociology of Social Control*, Aldershot, Gower.

_____ (1987b) 'Taking realist criminology seriously', *Contemporary Crises* 11: 371–401.

_____ (1989) 'Privatisation in perspective', in R. Matthews (ed.) *Privatising Criminal Justice*, London, Sage.

May Committee (1979) *Report of the Committee of Inquiry into the UK Prison Services*, Cmnd 7673, London, HMSO.

Millard, D. (1982) 'Keeping the probation service whole: the case for control', *British Journal of Social Work* 12.

Mnookin, R. and Kornhauser, L. (1979) 'Bargaining in the shadow of the law', *Yale Law Review* 88: 950–97.

Moore, C. and Meithe, T. (1986) 'Regulated and unregulated sentencing decisions: an analysis of first-year practices under Minnesota's felony sentencing guidelines', in *Law and Society Review* 20, 2: 251–77.

Moore, P. (1981) 'Scroungermania again at the DHSS', *New Society* 22, January: 138–9.

Morgan, R. and Bowles, R. (1981a) *Fines Project – Home Office Interim Report*, unpublished.

—— (1981b) 'Fines: the case for review', *Criminal Law Review*, 203–14.

Morris, N. (1974) *The Future of Imprisonment*, Chicago, Ill., University of Chicago Press.

Morrison, G. (1985) 'Small is beautiful? Observations on the Dutch Penal Service', *Journal 59* July: 2–7.

Moss, N. (1989) *Tackling Fine Default*, London, Prison Reform Trust.

Moxon, D. (1983) 'Fine default, unemployment and the use of imprisonment', *Home Office Research Bulletin 16*, London, Home Office.

Mullen, J. (1987) 'State responses to prison crowding: the politics of change', in S. Gottfredson and S. McConville (eds) *America's Correctional Crisis*, Westport, Conn., Greenwood Press.

NACRO (1981) *Fine Default: Report of a NACRO Working Party*, London, NACRO.

—— (1983) *NACRO Briefing: The Day Fine*, London, NACRO.

—— (1986a) *Black People and the Criminal Justice System*, London, NACRO.

—— (1986b) *Enforcement of the Law Relating to Social Security*, London, NACRO.

—— (1988a) *The Costs of Penal Measures*, London, NACRO, May.

—— (1988b) *NACRO Briefing: The Electronic Monitoring of Offenders*, London, NACRO, July.

—— (1988c) *NACRO Briefing: Fine Default*, London, NACRO, September.

Nagel, W. (1977) 'On behalf of a moratorium on prison construction', *Crime and Delinquency* 23: 154–72.

NAPO (1983) *Fine Default and Debtors Prisons*, London, National Association of Probation Officers.

National Children's Home (1988) *Children in Danger*, London, National Children's Home.

Office of Fair Trading (1988) *Annual Report of the Director-General of Fair Trading 1987*, London, HMSO.

Parliamentary All-Party Penal Affairs Group (1980) *Too Many Prisoners*, London, HMSO.

Pashukanis, E.B. (1978) *Law and Marxism: A General Theory*, London, Ink Links.

Pease, K. and Wasik, K. (eds) (1987) *Sentencing Reform: Guidance or Guidelines?*, Manchester, Manchester University Press.

Petersilia, J. (1988) 'Probation reform', in J. Scott and T. Hirshi (eds) *Controversial Issues in Crime and Justice*, London, Sage.

Posen, I. (1976) *A Survey of Fine Defaulters and Civil Debtors in Pentonville*, unpublished.

Quinn, T. (1984) 'Focus for the future: accountability in sentencing', *Federal Probation* 48, 2, March: 10–18.

Reiman, R. (1979) *The Rich Get Richer and the Poor Get Prison*, 1st ed, London, Wiley.

—— (1984) *The Rich Get Richer and the Poor Get Prison*, 2nd ed, London, Wiley.

Rifkind, M. (1988) 'Prisons and penal society', *Scottish Office News Release* 25 January.

Rosenbaum, M. (1983) *Women on Heroin*, New Brunswick, NJ, Rutgers University Press.

Rusche, G. and Kirchheimer, O. (1939) *Punishment and Social Structure*, New York, Russell & Russell.

Rutherford, A. (1984) *Prisons and the Process of Justice*, Oxford, Oxford University Press.

_____ (1986) *Growing Out of Crime*, Harmondsworth, Pelican.

Ryan, T. and Ward, M. (1989) 'Privatisation and penal politics', in R. Matthews (ed.) *Privatising Criminal Justice*, London, Sage.

Sabine, B.E.V. (1966) *A History of Income Tax*, London, Allen & Unwin.

Sanders, A. (1988) 'The limits of diversion from prosecution', *British Journal of Criminology* 28, 4: 513–32.

Scheerer, S. (1986) 'Dissolution and expansion', in B. Rolston and M. Tomlinson (eds) *The Expansion of the European Prison System*, Working Papers in European Criminology, no 7, Belfast, The European Group for the Study of Deviance and Social Control.

Schneider, A. (1984) 'Divesting status offenders from Juvenile Court jurisdiction', *Crime and Delinquency* 30, 3: 347–70.

Schur, E. (1973) *Radical Non-Intervention*, Englewood Cliffs, NJ, Prentice-Hall.

Schwartz, I., Jackson-Beeck, M. and Anderson, R. (1986) 'The "hidden" system of juvenile control', *Crime and Delinquency* 30, 3: 371–86.

Scottish Home and Health Department (1987) *Prison Statistics, Scotland*, Statistical Bulletin 6/87, Edinburgh, Scottish Office Prison Statistics.

Scull, A. (1987) 'Decarceration reconsidered', in J. Lowman, R. J. Menzies and T. S. Palys (eds) *Transcarceration: Essays in the Sociology of Social Control*, Aldershot, Gower.

Serrill, M. (1975) 'Juvenile corrections in Massachusetts', *Corrections Magazine* 2: 3–40.

Shapland, J. (1981) *Between Conviction and Sentence*, London, Routledge & Kegan Paul.

Shaw, S. (1982) *The People's Justice*, London, Prison Reform Trust.

_____ (1987a) 'Privatisation and penal reform', in *Prison Report*, London, Prison Reform Trust.

_____ (1987b) *Conviction Politics: A Plan for Penal Policy*, London, Fabian Society.

Shenfield, A.A. (1968) *The Political Economy of Tax Avoidance*, IEA Occasional Paper no. 24, London, Institute of Economic Affairs.

Simmel, G. (1978) *The Philosophy of Money*, trans. D. Frisby, London, Routledge & Kegan Paul.

Singer, P. (1979) *Just Deserts*, Cambridge, Mass., Ballinger.

Smith, D., Blagg, H., and Derricourt, N. (1988) 'Mediation in the shadow of the law: the South Yorkshire experience', in R. Matthews (ed.) *Informal Justice*, London, Sage.

Smith, M. (1984) 'Will the real alternatives stand up?', *New York University Review of Law and Social Change* 12, 1: 171–97.

Smith, R. (1985) 'Who's fiddling?', in S. Ward (ed.) *DHSS in Crisis*, London, Child Poverty Action Group.

Snider, L. (1982) 'Traditional and corporate theft: a comparison of sanctions', in P. Wickham and P. Dailey (eds) *White Collar and Economic Crime*, Lexington, Mass., Lexington Books.

Softley, P. (1973) *A Survey of Fine Enforcement*, Home Office Research Study 16, London, HMSO.

_____ (1978) *Fines in Magistrates' Court*, Home Office Research Study 46, London, HMSO.

Softley, P. and Moxon, D. (1982) *Fine Enforcement: An Evaluation of the Practices of Individual Courts*, Research and Planning Unit Paper 12, London, HMSO.

South, N. and Scraton, P. (1981) *Capitalist Discipline, Private Justice and Hidden Economy*, Middlesex Polytechnic, mimeo.

Speed, D. (1987) 'The use of custody – have we got our priorities right?', *Justice of the Peace* 21: 743–5.

Stern, V. (1987) *Bricks of Shame: Britain's Prisons*, Harmondsworth, Penguin.

Sutherland, E. (1983) *White-Collar Crime: The Uncut Version*, London, Yale University Press.

Taxpayers' Charter (1986) London, Board of Inland Revenue/HM Customs and Excise.

Taylor, M. and Pease, K. (1989) 'Private prisons and penal purpose', in R. Matthews (ed.) *Privatising Criminal Justice*, London, Sage.

Tempo (1988) Department of Employment Group Staff Newspaper November.

Teubner, G. (1983) 'Substantive and reflexive elements in modern law', *Law and Society Review* 17, 2: 239–85.

Thomas, D. (1979) *Principles of Sentencing*, 2nd edn, London, Heinemann.

Thornstedt, H. (1975) 'The day fine system in Sweden', *Criminal Law Review*.

Tonry, M. (1987) 'Sentencing guidelines and sentencing commissions', in K. Pease and M. Wasik (eds) *Sentencing Reform*, Manchester, Manchester University Press.

Uglow, S. (1984) 'Defrauding the public purse', *Criminal Law Review* March, 128–41.

United Nations (1976) *Economic Crises and Crime*, New York, United Nations Social Defence Research Institute.

__ (1980) *De-Institutionalisation of Corrections and its Implications for the Residual Offender*, Sixth UN Congress on the Prevention of Crime and the Treatment of Offenders, Paper A Conf. 87/7, New York, United Nations.

US Department of Justice (1983) *Report to the Nation on Crime and Justice: The Data*, Washington, DC, Department of Justice.

Van Dijk, J. (1988) *'Penal Sanctions and the Process of Civilianisation'*, paper presented to 10th International Congress on Criminology, Hamburg.

Vennard, J. (1975) *Imprisonment for Non-Payment of Fines or Maintenance*, unpublished.

Von Hirsch, A. (1976) *Doing Justice*, New York, Hill & Wang.

__ (1986) *Past or Future Crimes*, Manchester, Manchester University Press.

Walker, A. and Walker, C. (1987) *The Growing Divide: A Social Audit 1979–1987*, London, Child Poverty Action Group.

Walker, N. (1976) *Treatment and Justice in Penology and Psychiatry*, Edinburgh, Edinburgh University Press.

__ (1980) *Punishment, Danger and Stigma*, Oxford, Blackwell.

Walker, N. and Hough, M. (1988) *Public Attitudes to Sentencing: Surveys from Five Countries*, Aldershot, Gower.

Wells, C. (1988) 'The decline of the English murder: corporate crime and individual responsibility', *Criminal Law Review* December: 788–801.

Wheeler, J. (1980) *Who Prevents Crime?*, London, Conservative Political Centre.

Wheeler, S., Weisburd, D. and Bode, N. (1982) 'Sentencing the white-collar offender: rhetoric and reality', *American Sociological Review* 47: 641–59.

Wheeler, S., Mann, K. and Sarat, A. (1988) *Sitting in Judgement: the Sentencing of White-Collar Criminals*, London, Yale University Press.

Wilkins, G. (1979) *Making Them Pay*, London, NACRO.

Wilkins, L. (1984) *Consumerist Criminology*, Aldershot, Gower.

Wilson, J. (1980) 'What Works? Revisited', *Public Interest* 61, fall: 3–17.

Wright, M. (1988) 'What the public wants', in M. Wright and B. Galaway (eds) *Mediation and Criminal Justice*, London, Sage.

Young, J. (1987) 'The tasks facing realist criminology', *Contemporary Crisis* 11, 337–50.

——— (1989) *Criminology, A Realist Critique*, London, Sage.

Young, P. (1987) *Punishment, money and the legal order: an analysis of the emergence of monetary sanctions with special reference to Scotland*, unpublished PhD thesis, University of Edinburgh.

——— (1989 forthcoming) *Punishment, Money and the Legal Order*, Edinburgh, Edinburgh University Press.

Author index

Subject index